Roofscape Design

T0311415

jovis

Roofscape Design

Regenerating the City
upon the City

Gustavo Ambrosini / Guido Callegari

Section I Re-designing the roof 7

Section II 24 Case studies 75

Section I
Re-designing the roof

Roofscape design: an introduction

Gustavo Ambrosini, Guido Callegari

There are several reasons that lead the roof – one of the main traditional elements of architecture – to gain renewed prominence in the discourse about city transformations. An important topic is related to the relevance of urban fabric resilience, as well as to the search for more sustainable development models aiming at reducing environmental impacts and waste of resources; the so-called "no net land take" approach offers new potential to the reuse strategies of city rooftops. The risks of land-consuming models and of the impoverishment of values in metropolitan communities have prompted a warning towards urban sprawl policies. The present-day narrative, based on more compact models, reflects the criticism against large-scale developments that arose in North America in the nineteen-sixties: it is intended as a response to the growing need to limit land consumption, and as a condition for ensuring social diversity and more sustainable transport systems. Some urban planning strategies are taking into account the upper level of the cities as a potential surplus in terms of usable areas, both for private and collective activities. In recent densification policies, special attention is paid to the roof as a sort of "raised ground," by checking its availability to support a (moderate) city extension, adding extra floor space for new functions or greenery. An "urban acupuncture" logic is envisioned, in which limited vertical extensions can provide small-scale interventions, so that to improve social and cultural values of the involved communities. It is a concept contrary to the sprawl models, oriented at reducing costs and waste of energy of new urbanization.

Furthermore, vertical extension should take a part in wider redevelopment policies for existing real estate, enhancing an increase in the life cycle of buildings. The renovation of ordinary, low-quality housing stock constitutes in fact one of the most urgent urban issues. It is a widely diffused phenomenon, more evident in European public housing districts built during the post-war industrial boom: they show a generally poor state of conservation, they lack thermal insulation of façades and windows, they require the installation of active and passive energy saving systems etc. One of the most common strategies is to make retrofit interventions; but the action of retrofitting existing estates, in order to improve energy efficiency, seems to put the emphasis on construction work as a purely technological matter. Instead, the current challenge consists in adopting an inclusive approach so as to avoid a separate attitude and to integrate the technical elements into the architectural identity issue.

In this framework, the roof should undergo great changes in terms of materials, function, and shape: the cover of the buildings can thus play a key role in strategies aimed at combining the improvement of energy and functional performances with the increase in the number of dwellings. Vertical extension scenarios thus constitute an increase in real estate values and thus meet the market demand: the economic increment deriving from the new additions should allow high retrofitting costs to be borne.

Alongside the policies aimed at improving residential real estate, the construction of new public places takes on significant value, too. Interventions for the vertical extension of buildings conceived for public or collective functions often exploit the possibility of a necessary improvement of energy efficiency and safety standards as a way of integrating the new activities within the urban network. This process is accompanied by specific directives at the international level, especially in Europe and the United States: these are policies aimed at extending the life cycle of existing buildings, promoting intervention of reuse and adaptation, and relating sustainability issues – such as energy conservation, reduction of materials consumption, etc. – with new development opportunities.

The book explores recent experiences based on intervention models, such as building-on and the integration of new volumes into existing structures. It provides a survey of worldwide case studies in order to define some recurring topics. The case studies illustrated here express a specific attitude that is to be distinguished from two opposing trends. On the one hand, the logic of a mere extension of the original fabric, conceived as a simple repetition of already existing spaces and forms. On the other hand, the superimposition of an autonomous object acting as a parasite on an existing building: experimental temporary architectures or art installations aimed at producing a strong contrast with the hosting body.

On the contrary, the relationships between the new intervention and the existing structure should refer to the concept of "mutualism," as a symbiotic relationship in which both partners benefit from reciprocal advantages: although different in terms of spatial logic and formal expression, the two components are dependent on and conditioned by each other. It is what is described in biology as a "reciprocal exchange of nutrients." In this sense, these projects belong to a symbiotic approach that exploits the extraordinariness of the "top condition" offered by the roof to promote a subtle change in the urban identity of the building as a whole.

It is necessary, in fact, to recall the great imaginative potential the roof has in the architecture of the city, thanks to its ambivalent character: from the status of a place to be looked at – the "fifth façade" of buildings – to a place that should offer a "new ground" to the city. A large roof painting that Alexander Calder realized in 1974 in Grand Rapids well exemplifies the first concept. Large spots of red and black paint on a white background were intended to lend a dynamic feature to the dull, flat surface of the 1,600-square-meter roof of the Kent County Administration Building, visible from the buildings around it; moreover, they establish a relationship with the red arching and curving forms of the monumental sculpture created by Calder himself a few years earlier in the nearby square. A pictorial approach that recurs in various experiences: from the geometric tiling composition that Victor Vasarely realized on top of the Monaco Congress Center in 1979 to the large paintings aimed at redeeming "forgotten" roofs carried out by various contemporary artists such as Ella and Pitr, 1010, BirdO and others.

The concept of the roof as a living space – like a ground for human activities – is a recurring theme in the architectural debate of the twentieth century. It is well known that Le Corbusier's codification of the roof garden as one of the "Five Points Towards a New Architecture" represented a significant aspect in the controversy in which "modern" flat roofs were contrasted with "conservative" pitched roofs.

A conceptualization of the roof in which converged the faith in technological progress and suggestions from hygienist theories and from "machine age" visions. Above all, a new status was established: a place to be used, from the concept of the simple extension of internal living space to the idea of a setting where the community can gather.

However, in relation to the theme of the imaginary, it is also necessary to think of the expressive capacity of the roof in involving the physical experience of the user. Thus, there are other experiences from the twentieth century that can clearly exemplify this theme. If we refer, for instance, to the works of Antoni Gaudí, we can find one of the most powerful images of the roof as a raised walkable architectural landscape in his Milà House in Barcelona. The top of La Pedrera is a continuous undulating path that varies in height and is punctuated by an exceptional composition of technical elements sculpted in anthropomorphic shapes: it enhances the organic essence of the building, providing a tactile sensation and a breathtaking engagement with the views of the city. Actually, in common perception, the imagery associated with the use of the roof is often conceived in terms of an extraordinary experience. A feeling that is amplified by cinematographic visions, in which the roof is very often depicted as "another place," distinct from ordinary reality. In hundreds of movies, the most iconic and emotional scenes, in fact, take place on the roof: chase scenes providing adrenaline-pumping camera sequences along roofscapes, intense action scenes causing a feeling of vertigo, intimate scenes enhancing dramatic, melancholy or enchanting atmospheres, dance scenes freeing energies from ordinary conventions. Finally, emotional urban performances were nurtured by rooftop concerts, like the pioneering ones by

Jefferson Airplane (1968) and the Beatles (1969), which were followed by many others. A space for the unusual, where extraordinary and surprising relationships between the human sphere and the surrounding world take place. From new public spaces to renewed housing estates, from private domains to shared communities, from reconquered pocket-size gardens to extensive farms, the roof space offers an extraordinary potentiality to architecture and to the town.

The twenty-four case studies presented in this book innovate traditional categories like housing, offices, and facilities by offering multiple ways of living, working, and recreating in the city. They challenge the reinvention of the characters of urbanity with different approaches. They test new technologies to set up lightweight and quick systems in order to deal with structural constraints and inhabited places. Several building typologies are involved.

Historical residential buildings. Rooftop redesign is intertwined with the more general instances of intervention in the historical heritage. It recalls the complex and articulated debate, which developed over the course of the twentieth century around the concept of restoration. The projects presented provide multiple approaches, all sharing the common matrix of refusing stylistic restoration, emphasizing the sense of intervention in existing heritage as critical action. It is possible to refer to some images from past projects to explore the disciplinary boundaries. The renovation of an apartment in the center of Vienna by Coop Himmelb(l)au appeared as a sort of built manifesto for renewing the historical city. The roof remodeling was based on wing-like skeletal elements bearing glazed panels that violently broke the continuous surface, producing a vivid tension

Rooftop Remodeling Falkestrasse, Vienna, 1983–88, Coop Himmelb(l)au

between roof and street. Considered as an emblem of the *Deconstructivist Exhibition* at MOMA in 1988, the project forced the constraints of the orthogonal references – as well as the limitation of building codes – to dynamically express the ongoing complexity.

The Didden Village project by MVRDV (2006) turned an individual space – the extension of a family residence – into an urban icon: the blue polyurethane volumes with pitched roofs, arranged to form a pattern of plazas and streets, create a village-like, abstract atmosphere on the roof of the building. The vernacular and stereotypical shape of a house reinforces the feeling of the demand for human-scale.

Rooftop redesign inside the traditional urban fabric thus generates a subtle change: even a scarcely significant extension should match spatial and constructive issues in order to push the limits of the livability concept of urban dwelling. It could also be a more substantial process of infilling the building volume by "excavating" inside it, leading to a complete renovation.

Didden Village, Rotterdam, 2002–06, MVRDV

Social housing complexes. Rooftop redesign could respond
to the growing need to improve energy and functional
performance of post-war neighborhoods, offering the
opportunity to add floor space while preserving existing
structures. It implies the possibility of adding a layered
city identity to those settlements apparently doomed to
an unchangeable future, such as massive public housing
estates. The need to avoid or to reduce relocation of residents
during refurbishment works leads to the use of cutting-edge
technologies, such as new prefabricated dry systems: the high
standards envisaged in the early stage of the project process
ensure short on-site building times. Modular lightweight and
prefabricated timber-based elements, often with integrated
building services and energy systems, are designed to provide
ready-to-assemble solutions for vertical extensions of housing
estates.

Factories reuse. Starting from the first interventions in the
United States in the mid-sixties – like the famous Factory
by Andy Warhol in New York and The Cannery in San
Francisco by Joseph Esherick – the reuse of industrial
buildings has become one of the most intriguing fields where

Tate Modern, London, 1994–2000, Jacques Herzog and Pierre de Meuron

to experiment the relationship between existing and new. In this sense, rooftop redesign often plays an important role, sometimes the most eye-catching component, in factory renovation processes. To introduce only some of the recurring approaches, we refer to a few well-known projects. Completion. When converting a former power station in London to accommodate the Tate Modern art gallery (2000), Herzog & De Meuron activated a subtle transformation strategy respecting the original architecture. The rooftop addition is a huge and bright glazed volume that gently complements the massive brick building: a horizontal "body of light," luminous at night, that provides the resting spaces, where people gather at the end of their visit, and a spectacular viewpoint over the city.

Lingotto Factory Conversion, Turin, 1983–2003, Renzo Piano Building Workshop

Counterpointing. The respectful conversion project of
the Fiat Lingotto factory in Turin by Renzo Piano in
the early nineteen-nineties was counterpointed by two
"foreign" volumes that have landed on the roof: the bubble-
shaped conference room – a glazed ellipse connected to a
cantilevered steel helipad – and the "Treasure Chest" picture
gallery, covered by a sophisticated canopy made up of layers
of profiled steel and glass plates. It pushes the limits of high
technology calling for extraordinariness, acting as an icon of
the company brand.

Subtraction. For the restoration of the Old Watermills in
Murcia (1984), Juan Navarro Baldeweg proposed a strategy
of excavation and addition. The redesign of the upper part of
the building made it possible to restore the original prismatic
shape of the lower part as a support for new, interconnected
sculptural volumes. The renewed complex should thus
activate a subtle understanding of the cumulative process of
historical stratification.

Service buildings. Finally, the vertical extension is a strategy
pursued to expand public buildings, like schools or spaces
for cultural activities. The case studies show how this
opportunity allows, on the one hand, to accommodate new
functions or to expand existing ones, and, on the other hand,

Restoration of the Old Watermills, Murcia, 1984, Juan Navarro Baldeweg

to recreate new special features in the interiors that are suitable to enhance the collective character of the buildings. To conclude, city roofscape redesign is here intended as an adaptive attitude, based on the knowledge of the dynamic process of transforming the physical realm. Far from a regressive preservation-only behavior, it represents a remarkable way of coping with urban regeneration issues. In this sense, rethinking the roof could put city identities to the test in order to provide a peculiar perspective on urban transformations.

The roof as a livable space: architecture and imagery

Gustavo Ambrosini

The landscapes of roofs

The theme of the upward expansion of buildings is inherent in the very idea of the city. Cities, and European ones in particular, can in fact be considered the result of the superimposition and juxtaposition of successive layers dating back to different historical periods. We are used to look at the urban context as a palimpsest: building structures and urban patterns undergo a continuous process of overwriting which makes their features appear mixed and hybrid. The last layer – the one we see from above – is a complex and yet unplanned landscape: a roof landscape, which is not immutable, and reveals, through its forms and objects, the traces of its own temporariness. The bird's eye view of the cities vividly represents the patterns of urban morphologies, and at the same time shows a domain subject to multiple changes, where conflicting demands for use coexist.

Seen from above, the space of the roofs looks like a pure technical space, punctuated by a series of anonymous and unpleasant objects: chimneys, pipes, fans, cooling units, tanks, television antennas and cell phone towers, solar and photovoltaic panels, billboards, etc. An uninhabited space, not designed for people. But beyond that, other objects seem to express the desire to reconquer this space for the human

Technical roof, Turin

Roof garden, Turin

sphere: shrubs, pergolas, gazebos, tents, deck chairs, extensive or vegetable gardens – spaces thus re-occupied by people in order to better inhabit their city.

These "hidden" uses of roof spaces are visible to everybody, thanks to the development of aerial photography: from the first pictures taken from a balloon in the second half of the nineteenth century to the photographic surveys made by the Fairchild Aerial Survey Company in the United States and by Aerofilms Ltd in Britain before and after World War II. Aerial photography followed the mutual advances in both photography and aviation, matching military and scientific purposes with the establishment of an aesthetic imagery of the city.

Today, the boundaries of the traditional domain to which aerial photography belongs are becoming somewhat blurred. On the one hand, high-flying professional photography is now being questioned by the diffusion of do-it-yourself photography, increasing because of the amateur use of drones; the technological improvement and the significant reduction in prices allows a wide access to high-flying remote-controlled cameras. Even a beginner may have the opportunity to get a great shot while capturing images from the above. On the other hand, since the launch of Google Earth in 2005, everyone can search and explore almost any roof in the world from the comfort of his own home, thanks to the pervasiveness of geo-browsers, by simply turning up and down the mouse wheel: the possibility to zoom through different scales so quickly gives the impression of moving within the space, providing users with a tangible and perceptual experience.

Nevertheless, the ways cities are visualized still owes a lot to high-flying professional photography. The great circulation of aerial photo books, for instance, has implied a change in the city's visual iconography. Since the starting in 1969 of Robert Cameron's popular *Above* series of "coffee table" photobooks, aerial city portraits became a widespread observation point of urban landscapes for everyone to enjoy, making them something more available and familiar.[1] Multiple approaches to representation emerged, which are far from any claim to objectivity, creating aesthetic imageries from the interpretation of human activities and environmental relationships. Among others, it is worth to recall the visual inventiveness of the *Site Specific* series by Olivo Barbieri, portraying densely inhabited urban environments around the world, intended to focus, literally, on the physical outcomes of the radical mutations of metropolitan forms.[2] We could also mention the aerial night views by Vincent Laforet that push the boundaries of artistic interpretation and represent the city centers as illuminated architectural morphologies, emerging between darker forms and expressing themselves as pure energy of lights, captured in clarity and detail.

However, the sharpest representations of how roofs are used can be found in the well-known works of Alex MacLean. In his book *Visualizing Density* (2007), he depicted an extensive portrait of roofscapes all over the United States, aiming to show the density of neighborhoods at many levels, together with the different planning and design strategies behind it. But it is his book *Up on the Roof: New York's Hidden Skyline Spaces* (2012) that offers the deepest insight into the use of the city's top level, which is invisible from the ground. MacLean's lens discovers the enormous potential of outdoor and indoor spaces above New York's buildings (not an ordinary city, it has to be noticed): basketball and tennis courts, cocktail bars and restaurants, playgrounds, pools, sunbathers, herbaceous borders, beehives, gardens, art installations, alongside the famous historical water towers. Places to meet people, to swim, eat, sunbathe, and farm. This work provides a sort of anthropological commentary on a hidden world, revealing an amazing complexity and livability. In the introduction, architecture critic Robert Campbell describes the rooftops as the "lungs of the denser city of the future (...) [that] will connect us with nature, with wind and sun and rain and snow, with the natural processes of growth and decay."[3]

Opposite imageries: top-down luxury versus bottom-up informal

The roof space is thus a non-ordinary space, which recalls multiple and somehow contradictory ways to perceive its potential: a vast and diversified sphere, with two opposing imageries at the two extremes. At one side, the concept of a roof as a luxury domain, where the elites enjoy exclusive experiences, a place celebrated in advertising with an abundance of superlative expressions, from "stunning private suite on the top floor" to "an oasis where you can feel the breeze on your skin, sip a drink and marvel at breath-taking panoramas." At the opposite side, the so-called informal use of the city, when residential settlements in precarious conditions are the result of illegal rooftop occupancy by poorest classes: autonomous and unauthorized communities that grow outside – literally on top of – the legal city.

To discuss the first model, it is worth noting that, from the late nineteenth century onwards, a fundamental technological progress occurred, enabling a complete revolution of the

building hierarchy that had characterized the historical city
over the centuries. In fact, the invention of the elevator made
it possible to completely overturn the vertical layering of the
city, where the hierarchical occupancy of the different levels
of the building represented the differences between social
classes – from the lower *noble floor* reserved for wealthier
families to the upper floors used by servants. Actually,
it was not the invention of the elevator itself – through
the centuries, rope and pulley systems had formed lifting
systems for construction purposes, and "ascending rooms"
were experimented with since the first half of the nineteenth
century – but the development of a particular technological
device: the automatic safety brake invented by Elisha G. Otis,
who presented it to the public at the New York World's Fair
in 1854 and patented it in 1861. Since the construction of the
Equitable Building in New York in 1870, considered to be
the first building in the world to be equipped with passenger
lifts, leisure and living spaces started rushing towards the top,
away from the dust and clamor of the city's streets.
The roof garden built in 1890 on top of the Casino Theater
at the corner of Broadway and 39th Street is considered the
first rooftop terrace in New York City, modelled on existing
public terraces in Paris: it accommodated a promenade with
winding pathways among planted flowerbeds, a café, and
spaces for concerts and performances. In the early nineteen-
hundreds, columnists defined the New York nightlife scene as
the "roof garden season," where high society could enjoy open
spaces on top of theaters – among them Madison Square
Garden and the Olympia, Victoria and Republic Theaters –
as planted fairylands for leisure. Their success was closely
linked to the fortunes of variety entertainment, and they
declined when the invention of the cinema caused them to

Tudor City, New York City, 1925–32, H. Douglas Ives, Fred F. French Company

fall out of fashion around World War I. But a general concept
had been established, and the quality of the elevated location,
far from the overcrowded city ground, was incorporated into
the architectural design of offices, hotels, and apartment
buildings.

The so-called penthouse apartments saw a huge increase
during the skyscraper construction boom in New York in the
nineteen-twenties. By moving laundry rooms and servants'
quarters from the attic to the basement, wealthy classes took
advantage of the possibilities of view, fresh air and privacy:
the will to emphasize status and prestige encouraged the
adoption of forms for the upper part of the building that were
distinct from the ones below. The setback from the vertical
face of the building or the use of flat rooftops provided

Marina Bay Sands, infinity pool, Singapore, 2006–10, Moshe Safdie

landscaped open spaces or terraces, high above the city's
ordinary streets. The flourishing of eclectic architectural
features, between Art Deco and historical revival, very often
aimed at representing the memory of the countryside mansion
in the new urban apartment buildings.
Nowadays, the link between luxury and the ostentation of
wealth, and the idea of exclusive architectures with exclusive
views, is best symbolized by typologies such as rooftop bars
and rooftop infinity pools. From pocket-size bars to spacious
restaurants with pools and gardens, they all share the
common character of having the best view from a building:
the architectural features, the furniture, the artificial lighting
are aimed at creating trendy ambiences, conceived to offer
users a sophisticated and thrilling experience, based on the

possibility to enjoy breathtaking vistas over the city skyline and landscape. Finally, the "infinity pool" is the element that most of all evokes the idea of exclusivity derived from the position at the top of a building: a seemingly endless stretch of water, apparently vanishing into the horizon. The creation of a disappearing-edge illusion offers the body the most unconventional experience. The act of stepping out of an ordinary condition is here a real physical act: one undresses and dives into the water, with the extraordinary feeling of "swimming" above the surrounding landscape – on top of a historical town, among a skyscraper skyline, into the sea in the distance, etc. The "infinity pool" constitutes an architecture purely devoted to relaxation and fun.

The opposite image of roof usage is the one related to the phenomenon of illegal occupancy of the rooftop of buildings for the construction of housing units, in particular in South Asian and African metropolises: spontaneous neighborhoods, conceived outside of formal planning and processes, without complying with building regulations. Self-designed, self-built, with poor-quality, recycled materials, self-connected to infrastructure networks, these settlements belong to the form of urbanization defined as informal settlement. This type of settlement requires double attention. On the one hand, it is necessary to study the forms of settlement, trying to grasp the instances and "tactics" through which people make use of space. On the other hand, it is recommendable to keep away from a fascination with bizarre or folkloristic aspects and to avoid a naïve enchantment towards what is spontaneous but unhealthy.

One of the most notorious cases has been documented in the book *Portraits from Above. Hong Kong's informal rooftop communities* (2008) by Rufina Wu and Stefan Canham. In

Sham Shui Po rooftops, Hong Kong

Hong Kong, the huge migration flows of low-income people and the lack of available land resulted in critical housing shortage, fostering the phenomenon of informal settlements. Many thousands of people settled as a community of dwellers on the flat roofs of several high-rise buildings in the central urban areas: these structures are built from all kinds of poor, recycled materials, exploiting every available space. The juxtaposition of these shelters gives shape to a sort of elevated shantytown.

In some cases, the overlap of new structures with existing ones shows a critical threshold, beyond which the technological, structural, and building services systems risk to collapse. For instance, in the capital of Mozambique, Maputo, the privatization of the housing stock at the beginning

of the nineteen-nineties led to a process of relocation of
collective spaces on the rooftops and in courtyards, which
residents have appropriated for their own use or for rent.
The unchecked connection to the buildings' already fragile
systems of power cables, water and sewage pipes provoked a
worsening of the overall physical conditions and threatened
to damage the stability of the existing structures. At the
same time, growing tensions arose from the transformation
of collective spaces into secluded ones, exacerbating the
deterioration of the social contract.

The Modern roof

One of the most powerful images associated with Modern
Movement issues is, undoubtedly, the roof garden: it is
perhaps the most successful of the famous "Five Points
Towards a New Architecture," published in 1926 by Le
Corbusier and Pierre Jeanneret. The new concept upends
the way the treatises on architecture throughout history
had addressed the roof. For centuries, it was intended as the
structural element with the task of enclosing the physical
space of a building and acting as a pure shelter. The new
status assigned to the roof, on the contrary, converts it into
an inhabitable space for people. The relationship among the
first two principles – "the supports" (*pilotis*) and "the roof-
garden" – entails a kind of displacement process that inverts
the traditional elements of architecture. The classic tripartite
division of podium, columns, and entablature is transformed
into another, still tripartite, order, shaped in accordance to
a different use of the space: the individual supports allow
the house to be raised to an intermediate level, detached

from the "dampness of the soil"; "the building plot is left to the garden, which consequently passes under the house"; the "roof garden will become the most favoured place in the building".[4] The codification of basic principles proceeds from a practical dimension – the solution of specific architectural design issues – in order to establish a theoretical framework: the questions are posed programmatically, with the intention of giving them a character of objectivity, as a basis for the elaboration of a new architectural vocabulary. However, the proposed approach goes beyond the mere linguistic aspect and takes on a strong innovative significance on the urban conception level: "roof gardens mean to a city the recovery of all the built-up area." The text focuses on technical questions – the potentialities of the flat cement slab and the water drainage solutions – in order to illuminate the new possibilities of concrete construction, leaving little room for emotions. It is in another text, *The Theory of the Roof Garden* (1927), that Le Corbusier expresses the feeling of experiencing the roof: "The sky was glimpsed from each corner; far away from the street you enjoyed an agreeable sensation of wellbeing and security."

It is possible to identify several different driving forces behind this new conception of the roof. One of them could be referred to the "machine age" suggestions. First of all, the reference is to be found in some urban planners and visionary thinkers who, from the end of the nineteenth century onwards, developed new urban concepts, including means of transport and flows of energy into the layered structures of the city. These weren't meant as totally new urban systems but as radical improvements, which still kept features of the existing city patterns. It's worth to recall the high-rise dwelling unit system named *Aérodomes* that Henri-Jules Borie proposed in 1865: he envisioned a new urban level positioned on top of tall residential blocks, accessible from buildings via an elevator system and horizontally connected through a network of pedestrian paths, which accommodated public institutions such as schools and churches. The visions of *The Cities of the Future* (1910) by Eugène Hénard matched aesthetic and perceptual issues with the "mechanics" of the urban street: his famous drawing of the "Future Street" proposed an underground, multilevel infrastructural system feeding the buildings, whose flat roofs were intended to put "an area equal to the area of the whole house into useful service." These terraces were envisaged to support gardens for the residents, and "in the near future they will be used as landing stages for aeroplanes."

Then, many critics have pointed out the borrowing, to Le Corbusier's architectural imagery, of elements from other disciplines such as engineering, shipbuilding, industrial and aircraft construction. Therefore, the influence of the image of the ocean liner concerned both the functional sphere – the metaphor of a symbiosis among architectural shape and mechanics, the rational concept of spatial organization – and the emotional one. The series of wide decks, platforms, and walkways offered the fascination of a model of open-air life, entertainment, and sport above high-density residential cabins.

The unhealthy conditions of the overcrowded industrial cities led to the development of hygiene theories in the late nineteenth and early twentieth centuries: the consequent growing demand for sanitary criterions gave birth to a new typology, the sanatorium, that transposed the new theory of health into architectural form. The Schaffhausen-Thurgau Sanatorium in Davos, designed by Otto Pflegard, Max Haefli, and Robert Maillart in 1907 with flat roofs and open terraces, became a prototype designed to meet the need for ventilation, sunlight, and hygiene. These new forms of architecture were conceived as a sort of equipment for protecting and enhancing the body: the main element was the sun terrace, as the sublimation of the idea of preventing illness and preserving health. Hygienism thus pushed the development of the principle of rooftop solarium and terrace type, as defined by Richard Döcker in his book *Terrassentyp* (1929): an external "room" for open-air activity and physical exercise, shaped in a way to receive abundant natural light, air, and sun, to be incorporated in the design of hospitals, schools, offices, and housing units.

Yet the basic condition that made possible the development of the flat roof was, of course, the technological advances in building materials and structures aimed at obtaining a waterproof surface. It was, for instance, thanks to the invention of volcanic cement, used as a covering layer, that master builder Carl Rabitz realized his own villa with a roof garden in Berlin, which he presented at the International Exposition of 1867 in Paris. Similarly, the pioneer of concrete construction, François Hennebique, built his own house in Bourg-la-Reine in 1903 as a veritable manifesto of the new technology: the building seems to exhibit the strength and solidity of reinforced concrete, and its main feature is the suspended garden that covers the entire surface of the house, expressing the author's motto "flowers, light, and ventilation."

Arguments in favor or against the technical feasibility of the flat roof had a central role in the so called "controversy of the roofs" that arose in Germany in the nineteen-twenties. To support the new trends, in 1926 Walter Gropius launched

an international survey on the flat roof in the magazine
Bauwelt, involving some leading figures such as Behrens,
Döcker, Haesler, Hilberseimer, Hoffmann, Mendelsohn, Oud,
Taut, Van Loghem, and Le Corbusier. Five specific questions
were posed, focusing on the feasibility of technical solutions
regarding waterproofing, water drainage, heat insulation, etc.,
and explanatory drawings were requested. Le Corbusier, for
example, demonstrated how, in pitched roof houses, the snow
melted by modern heating systems overflowed the gutters
and then clogged them when it froze; he thus showed the
opportunity to retain the snow on a flat roof and to slowly
drain water from it through internal pipes. The emphasis had
been deliberately placed on the centrality of the technical
solutions, rather than on style, culture, or environment
matters. However, Gropius couldn't avoid writing that a "cubic
arrangement with horizontal roof surfaces is a recognized
mark of modern design in many projects and buildings of the
best modern architects of all nations."[5] A reaction came from
a conservationist position, intending to preserve a national
identity based on cultural heritage tradition (Heimatschutz),
with a counter-questionnaire published by Paul Schultze-
Naumburg in 1927: pitfalls due to the poor realizations of flat
roofs were highlighted, but above all the cultural relevance of
pitched roof tradition was discussed.
The flat roof easily appeared as a common trait that recurred
in different "modernisms," rejecting the stylistic eclecticism
of the nineteenth century. When planning the Werkbund
exhibition at Weissenhof in Stuttgart in 1927, artistic director
Mies van der Rohe established the use of a flat roof as a
rule. The idea of new style called for both a new modern
architecture and society: in *Das neue Frankfurt* magazine,
Ernst May published several essays in defense of the flat

roof by mentioning "an ethical force" as "a new, living expressive form"[6]; a shared unity in housing, expressing the idea of a shared unity in the society. Against the backdrop of conservative reactions, political and racial issues started to arise. Not surprisingly, one of the pretexts was the criticism of "orientalist" modern architecture – as expressed in the notorious faked mocking picture of the Weissenhof district as an "Arab village" published in 1934 – which reversed the value that modernists attached to the use of the flat roof in vernacular buildings of Mediterranean and Oriental tradition, as appeared, for instance, in Le Corbusier's travel sketchbooks.

The representation techniques used by Le Corbusier play a strong role in demonstrating the potential space of the habitable roof. The use of the axonometric view puts the garden roof in the foreground, enhancing its compositional value as a fifth façade; the use of the sketch depicts it as a room in the house where it seems as if the ceiling has been removed, freeing the view and breath towards infinity: the most dynamic room of the house for entertainment activities, as represented, for instance, in the movie *L'Architecture d'aujourd'hui* (1929) directed by Pierre Chenal. The physical features of the flat roof retain a multifaceted, not a homogeneous, character, in keeping with the different aesthetic expressions in Le Corbusier's work over the course of his life, following a kind of progressive detachment from the interior space. It provided a solarium, intended as an open-air extension of private domestic space, like in the first studies for the series of Citrohan houses in 1920, in the projects for a university residence ("with a corner to gaze at the stars"[7]), and for Villa Meyer in Paris in 1925, Villa Stein-de-Monzie in Garches (1927) and many others.

Villa Savoye, Poissy, 1928–31, Le Corbusier and Pierre Jeanneret

The flat roof became the climax of the architectural promenade in Villa Savoye (1928–31), revealing the final steps of the ascending path that connects the rooms along a continuous sequence: a two-level terrace, comprising the outdoor terrace bordered by the living spaces and the enclosure of the curved solarium crowning the house at the culmination of the ramp.

It acted as a sort of machine of vision in the de Beistegui attic in Paris (1930): the internal spaces and the three terrace levels were designed to offer an intimate and surreal experience, illuminated by the use of some electrically operated sliding framing devices and a periscope camera; on the top, white plastered walls partially obstruct the view of city monuments in the distance and surround a grass carpet

Unité d'Habitation, Marseille, 1947–52, Le Corbusier

under the open sky, unexpectedly furnished with a false fireplace with a mantelpiece, living room furniture and a mirror.

The flat roof constituted the main communal space of the Unité d'Habitation in Marseille (1947–52), a place physically and formally distinct from the residential sphere below it, where residents could gather or exercise. It is a podium punctuated by an articulated composition of rough concrete sculptural objects, pointing toward the sky, reminiscent of the silhouette of an ocean liner: the kindergarten, the gym, the shallow paddling pool for children, and the tall ventilation stacks shape an artificial landscape of abstract objects, meant to express the idea of social livability of the roof.

Architectural metaphors

Today there is a wide number of design experiences focusing on the exploitation or the reuse of the terminal part of a building as a livable space. To outline a first interpretative hypothesis, it is possible to identify some useful metaphors for reflection on many recurring attitudes. They are not univocal concepts, but sometimes ambiguous ones. Some of them are contradictory to each other. References to some projects from masters of twentieth-century architecture are cited hereafter to introduce the topics.

Distance

The first category should be related to the idea of detachment from the ground. In this sense, the Wolkenbügel by El Lissitzky of 1924–25 can be considered one of the

Wolkenbügel, 1924–25, El Lissitzky

forerunners of many utopian monuments of technological
progress designed in the course of the last century. His never-
built "sky-hook" was designed as a huge cantilevered slab
supported by fifty-meter-high piers to provide habitable space
above busy intersections of radial and ring roads in Moscow.
Featuring a horizontal layer far away from the ground,
figuratively detached from the functional support, it expressed
a separated urban habitat defying the law of gravity.[8]
Many mega-structural dreams of the nineteen-sixties owe a
lot to it. For instance, Yona Friedman's Ville Spatiale (1958–
62) was based on the idea of expanding the city by building
above it a gigantic structural skeleton supporting housing and
working units. Or the huge volumes hovering above cities or
natural landscapes drawn by Superstudio, as the Continuous
Monument of 1969, and the New Artificial Ground Layer for
Dusseldorf designed by Wimmenauer, Szabo, Kasper & Meyer
in the same year.
Among the closest realization to the constructivist model to
be mentioned is the Ministry of Transportation (now Bank
of Georgia) built in Tbilisi, designed by George Tschachawa
and Zurab Dschalagonia in 1975: a monumental complex
consisting of five mutually interlocked concrete blocks of two
stories each, appearing to be stacked on top of each other
and suspended from three vertical cores. Or the "Tree of Life"
housing complex built in 1994 by Fruto Vivas in Lechería,
Venezuela, in which several three-stories rectangular volumes
intersect and overlap each other as if they were floating in
the air, supported by slender columns made of steel sheet
sculptural forms.
It is a strategy of detachment that resonates in recent
realizations, such as, among others, the pixelated raised box
of the Sharp Center in Toronto by Alsop (2004), resting on

Ministry of Transportation (now Bank of Georgia), Tbilisi, 1975, George Tschachawa and Zurab Dschalagonia

colored bending pillars twenty-six meters above a small-scale streetscape; or the Antwerp Port House completed by Zaha Hadid Architects in 2016, in the shape of a diamond-like glazed volume floating above a nineteenth-century building. One of the most extreme examples of this approach to be cited is the Marina Bay Sands in Singapore, completed in

Marina Bay Sands, Singapore, 2006–10, Moshe Safdie

2010 according to the design by Moshe Safdie. Three fifty-seven-story towers support a transversal, boat-shaped volume that measures more than one hectare and cantilevers out sixty-five meters on one side, 200 meters above the city, hosting restaurants, cafés, trees, and a long pool. It appears as a monumental icon of a luxury microcosm, an alternative to the metropolitan spaces below.

Raising ground

On the opposite side, one can point out the approach of dealing with the roof as if it were part of the ground: the upper part of the building is modeled and given a sculptural form, providing a stage for human activities in direct connection with the landscape. Raising the ground as a folded surface becomes the main dispositive.

Historians recall Alvar Aalto's link between his travel sketches and the making of his own architecture and urban designs. The representation of the ancient theatre ruins as an element that fits into the landscape and at the same time re-defines it – a place of gathering with an artificial geometric order but in some way humanized by erosion process – is strongly linked to the open concavity of the auditorium of the university center in Otaniemi. With its fan-shaped plan and terraced profile it constitutes the focal point of the complex: the ground merges with a sloping roof in the form of a grandstand, giving form to an architectural landscape artefact, conceived for the gathering of people.

The main feature of Villa Malaparte, built by Adalberto Libera on the Isle of Capri in 1938, is undoubtedly the roof terrace: reverse pyramidal stairs without rails allow ascent

Otaniemi University of Technology, 1949–66, Alvar Aalto

Villa Malaparte, Capri, 1938–43, Adalberto Libera, Curzio Malaparte

to the sundeck, towards the view of sky and sea, and at the same time it acts as a theater facing the island's panorama with plants and rocks. The pure geometrical red volume thus achieves a harmonious relationship with the landscape. Only a white plastered curved wall counterpoints the flat roof and provides a hidden place encompassing nothing but the view to the horizon.

A perfect stage for the enactment of human drama, as admirably captured by Jean-Luc Godard in his 1963 movie *Le Mépris*.

Many contemporary projects can exemplify how materials enhance the physical experience of the accessible roof, the way people interact with it, by touching, stomping, or sitting on it; that space is devoted to both stay and circulation, possessing a dynamic feature.

Wood is the main material of the Yokohama International Passenger Terminal, designed by Foreign Office Architects

Cruise Terminal, Yokohama, 1995–2002, Foreign Office Architects

in 1995 and opened in 2002. A series of wooden folded surfaces, mixed with some grass ones, where the inside elements naturally flow towards the outside, provide a strong tactile feeling: people experience the building by walking, climbing, and lying on the upper deck, and also by "navigating" the internal pathways and ramps along three levels.

Brick tiles unify the upper surface of the Fiumicino City Hall by Alessandro Anselmi, completed in 2003: a mineral envelope rises from the street level, curves over the council chamber, and tilts to cover the office buildings. The symbolism inherent in the idea of a civic place is declined through the action of folding and cutting the surfaces, thus obtaining a segmented oblique plane: blending the traditional elements of architecture – the floor, the façade, and the roof – transforms the building itself into a public square.

Stone characterizes the appearance of the Oslo Opera House by Snøhetta (2007) as an architectural pathway, made of inclined pedestrian areas paved like urban streets, connecting the sea level to the upper terrace. The roof of the building

Oslo Opera House, 2000–07, Snøhetta

becomes a sloped urban geometry: the contrast with the transparent vertical glass façades, that allow views from and into the interior, illuminates the idea of a gathering place and open public building.

Naturalizing roof

One of the most current subjects regarding roof reuse today is the so-called "green roof": from low-maintenance and self-sustaining extensive systems to intensive ones, with a wide range of vegetation, from herbaceous plants to small trees, and advanced irrigation methods. Potential benefits of green roofs are widely recognized in terms of rainwater management, biodiversity preservation, reduction of the urban heat island effect, building insulation, air quality and acoustics improvement, aesthetics and quality of life, urban agriculture, etc.

Greening the roof involves architectural design in several respects. To briefly introduce this issue, it is useful to recall the tension between nature and artifice expressed in the roof garden project by Roberto Burle Marx for the Ministry of Education and Health in Rio de Janeiro (1938), a building designed by a team of architects leaded by Lucio Costa with Le Corbusier as consultant. In contrast with the straight "rational" lines of Le Corbusier's modernism, Burle Marx proposed to cover the lower wing of the building with sinuous and meandering masses of vegetation, reflecting the features of the tropical landscape: organic forms, textures, and vivid colors thus add a dynamic feeling. His sensitivity as a painter, combined with a deep knowledge of Brazilian flora, produced a set of vegetation that encompassed not just the visual

Olivetti West Residential Estate, Ivrea, 1968–71, Roberto Gabetti and
Aimaro Isola, with Luciano Re

sphere but also touch, fragrance and the changing features of
the seasons.

The relationship between nature and artifice is not a new
topic, but this somewhat archaic theme is made even more
urgent today by technological development. This matter is
put into question by a huge number of projects that have
explored the potentialities of realizing green roofs, expressing
a multiplicity of attitudes. Hereafter, only some of them are
outlined.

Searching a mimetic attitude with the landscape. In the
Olivetti residential center in Ivrea by Roberto Gabetti and
Aimaro Isola (1971), while the rear side is sunk into the
ground, the front elevation faces a wooded hill describing a
semi-circle around it, almost like an amphitheater: the convex
façade is hidden by a green cover that is partially paved. The
flat roof becomes a walkable extension of the surrounding

Fukuoka Prefectural International Hall, 1995, Emilio Ambasz

land. Mimesis is not intended as a concealment, but arises from a caring approach to the landscape, which interprets the building as a fragment that forms part of a general system. Providing an icon for the "re-naturalization" of the city. Emilio Ambasz's project of the Fukuoka Prefectural International Hall (1995) extends an existing park through a sequence of fifteen landscaped terraces, featuring gardens for meditation and relaxation, up to a wide belvedere on the top level. The stepped profile of garden terraces is home to tens of thousands of plants, which create a lush cascade of vegetation reminiscent of the ancient hanging gardens of Babylon.

Creating a playful representation of nature. The Hundertwasser House in the center of Vienna (1986) is an apartment complex, made of curved, irregular-shaped structures and undulating roofs covered with trees and

Hundertwasserhaus, Vienna, 1983–85, Friedensreich Hundertwasser with Joseph Krawina

California Academy of Sciences, San Francisco, 2000–08, Renzo Piano Building Workshop

shrubs. Lush greenery covers the entire roof surface and towers upon the flowing façades, which are made up of multiple textures of colors and windows of different sizes, combining pictorial art and environmentalism in the creation of an organic vision for the city.

Acting as a smart garden. The California Academy of Sciences building in San Francisco by Renzo Piano (2008) is rectangular in plan but undulates in section towards the center to form a series of rising domes of various sizes, covering the main exhibition areas. Thermal inertia significantly cools the interior, biodegradable coconut-fiber containers host autochthonous plants, skylights automatically open and close for ventilation, weather stations monitor wind, rain, and temperature, photovoltaic cells are installed between the transparent canopy around the perimeter. The roof acts as a sustainability-driven garden.

1   The *Above* series comprises nineteen volumes of aerial photographs, each of them portraying one city or natural area; the first one was Robert Cameron, *Above San Francisco* (San Francisco: Cameron and Company, 1969).

2   Olivo Barbieri's *Site Specific* series is a project started in 2003 to portray over forty cosmopolitan cities from above; the first one was Olivo Barbieri, *Site Specific_ROMA 04* (Roma: Zone Attive, 2004).

3   Alex MacLean, *Up on the Roof: New York's Hidden Skyline Spaces* (New York: Princeton Architectural Press, 2012).

4   Le Corbusier and Pierre Jeanneret, *Almanach d'architecture moderne*, Collection de "L'Esprit nouveau" (Paris: Éditions Crès, 1926), trans. Ulrich Conrads, *Programs and Manifestoes on 20th-Century Architecture* (Cambridge, MA: The MIT Press, 1970).

5   Walter Gropius, "Das flache Dach: Internationale Umfrage", *Bauwelt* (February–April 1926), cited in Richard Pommer, "The Flat Roof: A Modernist Controversy in Germany", *Art Journal* 43, no. 2 (1983): 158–69; "Revising Modernist History: The Architecture of the 1920s and 1930s", 107.

6   Ernst May, "Das flache Dach", *Das neue Frankfurt*, I, 7, (October-December 1927), cited in Richard Pommer, "The Flat Roof: A Modernist Controversy in Germany", 158–69.

7   Le Corbusier, *Towards an Architecture*, [1928] trans. John Goodman (Los Angeles: Getty, 2007), 286.

8   "The idea of the conquest of the substructure, the earthbound, can be extended even further and calls for the conquest of gravity as such. It demands floating structures, a physical-dynamic architecture.", El Lissitzky, *An Architecture for World Revolution*, [1929] trans. Eric Dluhosch (Cambridge, MA: The MIT Press, 1970).

Vertical extension as a strategy for the resilient city

Guido Callegari

The crisis as a (re)starting point

Some terms such as vertical extension, upward extension, additional stories, extending upwards, building heightening and roof ridge elevation express strategies being internationally developed and experimented as a means of expanding cities by building on roofs and top stories. Analyzed in the wider context of the major challenges exacted by this historical period, vertical superelevation could be seen as the way forward in the conceptual development of a new model of urban settlement, and as an additional component of an ecosystem.

Climate change caused by mankind in the latter quarter of the twentieth century has generated an unprecedented environmental crisis, and economic growth and urbanization are amongst the key factors for possible change in modern and advanced countries. By 2050, about seventy per cent of the world's population will be concentrated in urban areas, and the reduction of carbon emissions will be one of the most crucial strategies for accompanying the growth of these vast settlements, while at the same time mitigating the impact of the effects of climate change.

Although the AEC sector[1] has been slow to adopt technological innovations and processes, it is now essential that urban and architectural projects incorporate the

reduction of carbon emissions in their development stages.
Buildings are responsible for more than forty per cent of
global energy consumption and a third of global greenhouse
gas emissions and have a considerable direct impact on the
environment, from the selection of raw materials during the
construction phase, to the processes used in the production
and assembly of the components, the construction systems,
and the subsequent phases of maintenance and requalification
of the buildings throughout their life cycle. Infrastructures
and buildings worldwide use sixty per cent of the raw
materials extracted from the lithosphere, and of this overall
volume of resources, buildings represent forty per cent, that is
twenty-four per cent of all global extractions.[2]
As highlighted in the McKinsey Foundation report, large-
scale projects generally demand twenty per cent more
resources for their completion than initially estimated and
may exceed the preliminary budget by up to eighty per cent.
This reporting framework suggests that the construction
sector will have to make major changes if it intends to
pursue the aim of reducing energy consumption and carbon
emissions to minimum levels.[3]
While the concept of a low-carbon-emission city is closely
linked to sustainable development and represents one of
the most critical challenges of sustainability to be faced in
the coming decades, many countries have recognized the
implications of climate change and are gradually introducing
a range of policies and measures to lessen the negative trend.
The European Commission, in particular, has introduced
the European Green Deal, with the aim of making Europe
climate-neutral by 2050.
Existing European property assets cover approximately
twenty-four billion square meters and were mainly built

after the Second World War.[4] A considerable number of these buildings are residential and, having exceeded their life cycle, will have to be replaced or converted to meet the needs of a constantly changing society. In recent decades, the rapid and sprawling growth of urban settlements has given rise to an exponential increase in the consumption of land, with a multiplication of urban areas, altering (and in some cases abusing) the environmental systems. This real estate is the result of uncontrolled consumption of resources, and the urban planning was based on economic models which, in some cases, are no longer valid and reproduceable.
Which policies, processes, models, and resources can we use in the future to transform the existing real estate assets? How can we develop urban planning and architecture in the coming decades to encourage the passage from a linear economy to a circular one, introducing measures to mitigate

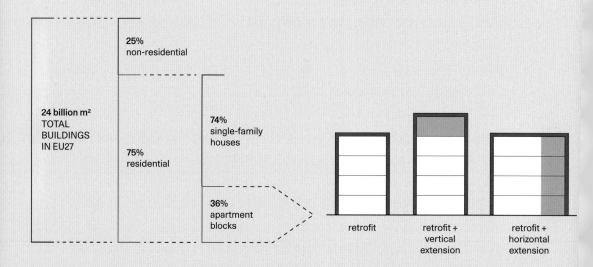

Figure 1_ This figure shows the gross floor area of existing buildings in Europe (UE-27 plus Norway and Switzerland) and the prevalent market share represented by apartment blocks (36%) to which retrofit, vertical extension, and extension strategies are currently being applied. In addition to the refurbishment of buildings by private owners, renovation of social housing by public bodies accounts for a significant share of the total.
[Source of data on the real estate area: BPIE Building Performance Institute Europe, 2011]

the effects of climate change, identifying new strategies for the densification of the cities in the face of the exponential increase in the world population, concentrated for the first time in history within urban settlements?

To deal with some of these complex challenges and encourage a genuine transition towards realistically sustainable cities, it will be necessary to enact a gradual experimentation of strategies capable of defining processes, in many cases unprecedented, compatible with the schedule for reconversion of consolidated practices and with the socio-economic models relating to the evolution of the cities.

Above all, in the industrialized countries with a low construction rate, the activities of the AEC sector will increasingly concentrate on refurbishment, retrofit, and deconstruction of existing buildings, and therefore the reuse of real estate will become one of the most important drivers of the market in relation to the various forms of sustainable urban development.

In order to spark the latent capacity of the reorganized models of intervention, it will be necessary to shift the center of interests and resources in favor of the conversion of existing real estate, in some cases initiating changes in use of extant urban structures with a creative approach in terms of design and process management.

The challenge of requalification: looking at urban real estate anew

Even in the past, as a center of economic and cultural development and social experimentation, the city was a vehicle for innovation, in many cases transforming the problems

and the criticalities into opportunities for change. This new
perspective will bring with it changes in the awareness and
the identity of entire areas of the city, through processes that
are often already underway in many European cities. In fact,
if we analyze the most recent period of history, we can see
architectural signs of a passage from a role as an industrial
city to a post-industrial one, increasingly dependent on light
industry, innovation, services, tourism, training, and processes
of economic transformation through the rethinking of the
identity of the places, dissolving the boundaries of certain
functions as they become irrelevant or altered. In some cases,
we see progressive reclamation of suburbs as integral parts of
the city; in others, the development involves the historic town
center with precise and limited processes of densification and
extension of the urban space by increasing the vertical density
or transforming derelict areas such as ex-industrial sites, ports,
military barracks, and factories. Through these processes
districts are reborn, with reorganization of the public spaces,
the infrastructures, and the transport system, extending the
interconnected areas for new forms of city life. In particular,
the passage from an industrial society to a society of
information opens up new possibilities for using the existing
infrastructures of the cities, the buildings, the roads, and the
supply structures, in a more modern and sustainable manner.
We are witnessing a process of experimentation and, in some
cases, the conversion of neighborhoods or the redevelopment
and extension of buildings through planning processes capable
of developing new methods of economic, social, cultural, and
political transformation, prevailing over the traditional legacy
of urban planning built on the presupposition of *tabula rasa*,
of the demolition and substitution of real estate, without
evaluating alternative theories.

The framework represented by the European cities, where the most ancient traces of the past are combined with the more recent thrust towards the future, is significant; a condition very different with respect to the frenetic growth according to other processes and other logics of the Asian cities and the Latin American metropolises. Nonetheless, the European cities preserve their relevance within the process of global change that is related to the present, and they are already projected towards the future.

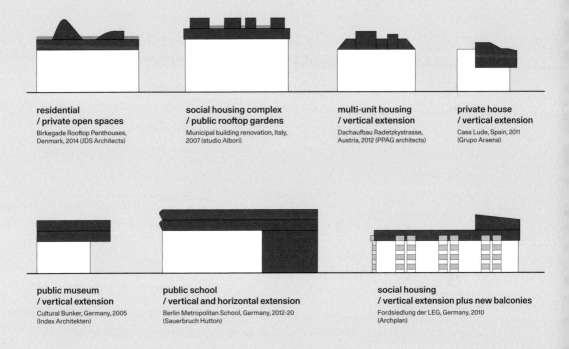

residential / private open spaces	social housing complex / public rooftop gardens	multi-unit housing / vertical extension	private house / vertical extension
Birkegade Rooftop Penthouses, Denmark, 2014 (JDS Architects)	Municipal building renovation, Italy, 2007 (studio Albori)	Dachaufbau Radetzkystrasse, Austria, 2012 (PPAG architects)	Casa Lude, Spain, 2011 (Grupo Araena)

public museum / vertical extension	public school / vertical and horizontal extension	social housing / vertical extension plus new balconies
Cultural Bunker, Germany, 2005 (Index Architekten)	Berlin Metropolitan School, Germany, 2012-20 (Sauerbruch Hutton)	Fordsiedlung der LEG, Germany, 2010 (Archplan)

Figure 2_ The comparison of seven case studies, including those analyzed and documented in this volume, summarizes the contexts in which building extension projects are carried out in inner-city development. Architectural additions to existing buildings, through vertical extension, extension, and infill, at times reflect the existing style and at others break completely with architectural traditions.

Although vertical superelevation is generally a very precise intervention, comprising private functions within the city, it sometimes also has collective or public functions, vitalizing the urban scene and adding architectural variety by reclaiming unused parts of the city, such as rooftops, with considerable potential for the use of space.

The challenge of the conversion and change of use of existing buildings also foresees the vertical superelevation of the cities, constituting an overlap between twentieth-century history and the new development practices for the urban settlements. In many cases, the new functions are located on roofs by integrating new living space with unused areas; and although vertical superelevation is generally a precise and highly individual intervention, comprising private functions within the rapidly changing cities, it is clear from the many case studies set out in this book that a number of vertically extended buildings have collective, public functions and in some cases tend to a vision of integration with the network of the urban structure. Thus, as in the past, the city continues to be a melting pot in which various forms of functional diversity for social inclusion merge with new urban and architectural strategies. Quite simply, the metamorphosis of the city starts with various presuppositions involving previously unused functional strata in a systematic manner. These approaches offer a range of possible creative transformations of the urban space with architectural additions to existing buildings through superelevation, extensions, and interpenetration of volumes that extend, combine, and redefine them thanks to a flexible vision, at times almost utopic if compared with the past, pursuing the aims of sustainable development. Frequently, the projects born from this vision are the expression of a break with the past, with provocative and self-referential approaches that give rise to contrasts with existing architecture by redefining the ways existing buildings are used. In other cases, a continuous interaction with the existing heritage is constructed through interpretations coherent with the function and the legacy of architectural and urban problems through a new reading.

In other situations, the premise is the redefinition of the functions of the city; for example, the residential districts reflecting an industrial past, which have changed over time to become a hub of urban vitality and architectural variety, reconquering part of the city with new functions and potential utilization.

We can therefore assume that, while the changes in the cities are a complex issue, they only apparently belong to a specialist and sectorial field of interest, since in the future these changes and this work will involve the awareness and the identity of a vast range of people. The meaning of the term 'change' to which we are referring therefore belongs not only to a technical dimension for insiders, such as decision-makers, technicians, planners, and investors, but also to the cultural dimension of those who live and work within the city, recognizing and repositioning the elements of value, and constructing new relations between the material environment and the designed and built space. The processes underway not only center on the potential represented by the conversion of the existing real estate, but above all on a new idea of 'city' that starts with an ecosystem designed to involve a new social vision of the urban dimension and the various functions associated with it. Therefore, while it is true that urban life has always been conditioned by the interactions between the processes of economic, social, geographic, political, and cultural change, nowadays these transformations are increasingly linked to a framework of epochal changes, which demand new trajectories of work and experimentation.

Growing upwards: policies, models, and experimental models for the expansion of the city

The culture of a city and its various expressions through architecture and construction culture can offer an extraordinary contribution to dealing with the challenges deriving from the demographic and economic changes underway, defining the operational practices for the coming decades in order to leave behind the paradox of wanting to pursue sustainability without having defined a complete and feasible model of a sustainable city.[5]

So, nowadays, the model of sprawling urban areas is counterposed with models of compact cities, with the aim of promoting more efficient use of resources, reducing the environmental impact, and improving the economic efficiency of processes deriving from high financial costs for the maintenance of infrastructures and collective services. The accelerated and expansive growth of urban territories is the result of urban planning based on economic models which, in some cases, are no longer feasible and repeatable. The need for more sustainable work trajectories therefore determines new logics of urban planning, within which falls the topic of vertical extension.

One expression of this trend is the *règles de construction d'extension vers le haut* of the City of Paris[6], which, given the lack of available land, has identified the superelevation of existing buildings as a sustainable and innovative solution to be encouraged, in order to meet the ambitious aim of producing 10,000 residential units per year. The regulations drawn up as part of the *Consultation Internationale du Grand Paris* (2008–09), whose findings were later included in the 2014 publication from the *Atelier Parisien d'Urbanisme* (Apur), analyzed the capacity for development of Parisian buildings, concentrating in particular on buildings located along wide streets or on corner lots, reaching the conclusion that almost ten per cent of the plots of land in Paris were suitable for superelevation of the buildings in relation to the streets.[7] The regulations also emphasized the advantages of this policy from a financial, architectural, and ecological standpoint, highlighting the fact that the practice of superelevation has been part of Parisian architectural history since the seventeenth and eighteenth centuries. The model of a compact city is feasible thanks to a change in the regulations and, in particular, the abolition of the *règle de densité* (COS) introduced by the ALUR law in March 2014 and the Duflot decree of October 2013. The legislation therefore encourages the construction of new buildings, without increasing the land area occupied by the buildings.

Although it starts from different premises, in 2020 the British government issued laws and regulations designed to redevelop the urban centers with the possibility for owners to build two additional stories on their property, in order to create new apartments, vital space for growing families, with swift planning permission procedures. In August 2020, the *Town and Country Planning Regulations 2020*[8] were approved, which allowed the extension of apartment buildings by adding two more stories. The existing building is required to have three or more floors before the extension is built and cannot be more than thirty meters tall when completed. In order to assist and facilitate property owners in redevelopment and vertical extension projects, the Ministry of Housing, Communities and Local Government has produced a technical guide entitled *Permitted Development Rights for Householders*.

Similarly, in Spain, since 2010, the bilingual *Libro blanco de la sostenibilidad en el planteamiento urbanístico español* (White Book of Sustainability in Urban Planning) by the Social and Economic Committee and the Housing Ministry criticized low-density urban models, widespread since 2008, proposing a compact city model to reduce environmental impact and improve economic efficiency deriving from the high cost of construction and maintenance. In this framework, the vertical extension of existing buildings has been explored as a solution to capitalize the available building land, characterized by very old buildings and, at the same time, as a vehicle for stimulating the redevelopment of the existing real estate, improving energy-efficiency and safety standards.[9]

The hypothesis of the upper level of the cities as a potential residual area for building therefore determines a new logic of urban planning, according to which the new functions, both private and collective, can be located on the roofs using processes that, with the necessary funding, could facilitate the redevelopment of the existing real estate. This perspective of expanding the cities appears more sustainable compared with the sprawl of the past, since it can be realized with less use of energy and cost savings for urbanization, incorporating the added value represented by an increase in the life cycle of the existing real estate, which would otherwise have to be demolished and replaced. The integrated approach to the improvement of existing buildings and vertical extension thus introduces a new management model for the planning process, according to the new market logic.

If we examine the legislation from other European countries, it is possible to see how the city that grows and is organized by functional strata represents a new paradigm of the 'feasible city,' thanks to new legislation and regulations capable of stimulating the market through processes that are both possible and essential. Therefore, the challenge of redevelopment and of vertical extension is not only technical, it is also fiscal and procedural and must be investigated from this standpoint.

In the last twenty years, Europe has laid down the operational premises for encouraging the development of existing buildings by planning structural funds and European investment. In the periods 2007–13 and 2014–20, the European Union set aside resources and enacted numerous programs and research projects with the aim of constructing an informative framework for the processes of real estate development, the identification of financial schemes suitable for the retrofit of social housing, and the development of more efficient ways of measuring the energy efficiency of residential buildings. The European strategies and policies deriving from this season of experiences and researches have become fundamental for enacting and inspiring the development of this emergent market, at the same time highlighting innovative technologies and processes for the realization of increasingly efficient interventions from economic and environmental standpoints. In some cases, prototypes of vertical extensions were developed, such as the SOLTAG project[10] in 2005, included in the EU's *Sixth Framework Programme* as a response to the vertical expansion of Copenhagen, placing 84m² apartments on flat-roofed apartment buildings in the nineteen-sixties and nineteen-seventies using an off-site process. The idea behind the project was that of a parasitical relationship between the new, more efficient and sustainable city, compared with the existing one, which was to be used as the foundation strata. This relationship between the old buildings and the new units was characterized by a state of necessity and interdependence. The *Sustainable Roof Extension Retrofit for High-Rise Social Housing in Europe* (suRE-FIT) project included in the EU's *Sixth Framework Programme* thanks to cooperation between various European partners, analyzed the technical, legislative, and economic limits and the capacity for vertical extension and augmentation of social housing as part of a wider strategy of urban redevelopment and regeneration.[11]

The research analyzed the redevelopment of social housing, concentrating on the technologies, methods, and procedures which made it possible to refurbish and extend the stock of existing homes, combining energy-saving measures and social, technical, and economic objectives. On the basis of a detailed analysis of experience already realized in Europe, the research set out criteria for planning and guidelines for the application of retrofitting solutions and interventions on the upper stories, highlighting the positive aspects. Amongst these, the adaptation strategy determines the creation of new residential units without building on new urban plots, improvement in energy efficiency, and the location of local services and communal spaces within the new volumes. The various strategies for intervention are classified as three main types – contrast / extension / integration – and were later applied to the development of pilot projects.

Alongside the experimental projects included in the European programs, there were national experimental programs developed in particular to improve social housing. Amongst these was the French national *program réhabilitation lourde des logements, un levier de la qualité architecturale, urbaine et environnementale* (REHA)[12] which, through a global approach to redevelopment, aimed to organize the interventions necessary to attain energetic, environmental, and comfort standards equivalent to new-builds, together with renewal of the architectural standards and sustainable urban refurbishment solutions. The existing residential buildings represent more than seventy per cent of the national buildings and are therefore an important aspect of the French policies with regard to commitment to ecological transition, with their refurbishment being an essential element. The main objective of REHA is the redevelopment of social housing and, through public competitions, it has invited multidisciplinary teams of professionals and project management companies to present proposals for innovative, scalable solutions with low carbon emissions. Through the research and analysis of redevelopment pilot projects, REHA aims to develop the knowledge base and create tools so that these operations can be organized according to their planning, financial, contractual, legislative, and legal dimensions. Two competitions were organized[13], which led to the authorization of numerous redevelopment case studies, and REHA has revealed the undeniable environmental benefits and economic opportunities: 10,000 homes redeveloped with an overall performance objective represent 800 million euros of work generated, 100 GW/h/year of energy saved, that is the GHG equivalent of 3,000 inhabitants. Over the years, REHA has organized the planning and management experience of the processes, constructing an important information framework to guide future interventions for sustainability of the investments.

Among the many experimental processes within the French REHA program and similar programs developed in other European countries, vertical extension has become the fulcrum of a planning process that also foresees the retrofitting of the interiors of residential units. In fact, the activities for the redevelopment of the existing buildings are not limited to external architectural upgrades, to the 'skin' of the buildings, but often give rise to a more complex process that involves the reorganization of the internal distribution of apartments, the transformation of balconies and loggias into bioclimatic greenhouses, and regulatory compliance of systems, communal spaces, and vertical connections, with

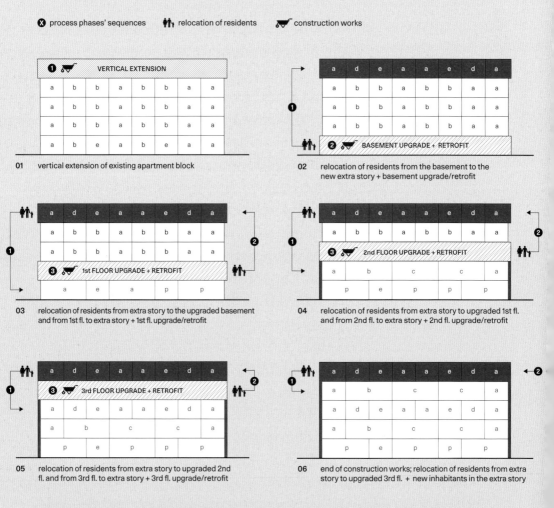

Figure 3_ In some cases, redevelopment of existing buildings demands planning and management of complex processes, involving communal spaces or private areas, with the consequent temporary relocation of residents. This figure summarizes the management phases of some European national programs for the redevelopment of social housing, where vertical superelevation became an essential 'filter space' for the complex residential rotation of the occupants. For this reason, the upwards extension of the building was the first work carried out in a complex project.

the addition of new lifts. In these cases, the vertical extension produces the residential units that become temporary spaces into which the residents are transferred (by rotation) while work is completed on their homes.

The various planning experiences of recent years have produced a set of new strategies, capable of enacting a program of interventions in phases, compatible with the needs of the users and the funding necessary for complex programs. The know-how gained from these experimental redevelopment sites makes it possible to analyze the impact of the management of the processes and their sustainability as investments.

The analysis of this dimension of the redevelopment process, that is the financial aspect, is of fundamental importance because there is a general lack of understanding of the processes and effective benefits in economic and social terms of the transformations and the potential prospects for innovation of new strategies among the stakeholders of the real estate market.

Therefore, the results of national programs are fundamental in drawing up international guidelines and frameworks to respond to the many questions still open regarding the models to be chosen. In the coming years it will be essential to implement knowledge of the impact and effects of the current research projects.

The intervention of vertical extension on social housing often affects the quality of life in small communities by inspiring other, more limited activities, which in turn may also encourage logics of 'urban acupuncture' through small-scale interventions that have considerable effects on social and cultural values, as in the case of Cinisello Balsamo, included in the studies analyzed in this publication.

Adaptive reuse: the driver for the development of new scenarios

While the preference for reuse and adaptation of existing buildings is an emergent trend internationally, this perspective also represents an opportunity for extending the useful life of existing buildings, supported by the key concepts of sustainability through reducing the consumption of materials, transport, energy, and pollution.

Experience has shown the benefits linked to both costs and environmental impact. As mentioned before, over the last twenty years Europe has undertaken a number of research projects with the aim of improving sustainable development, with particular emphasis on the question of the energetic efficiency of real estate. In the light of the challenges emerging, attention will be increasingly focused on the environmental aspects of the interventions, with particular reference to the impact incorporated in the buildings. Especially the energy incorporated in construction materials will be of importance, above all in a political framework that aims to move from a linear to a circular economy.

Although the energy used in the production phases of building components and the construction activities varies between ten and twenty per cent of the total energy consumption of a building, which during its life cycle will consume the majority of the energy, the consumption of resources for the production and transportation of materials will become central to the transition towards environmental policies capable of pursuing the objectives of the European Green Deal. In particular, prolonging the life of an existing building through reuse could reduce pollution and consumption of materials by using existing services and making a significant contribution to carbon reduction and sustainability. The process of reusing buildings will contribute considerably to the reduction of energy consumption, pollution, and waste, in contrast to the logic of demolition and substitution with new buildings and services. Therefore, the topic of vertical superelevation is nowadays seen as avantgarde compared with other topics of the circular economy, and in many cases the demolition and replacement of existing buildings may not be the

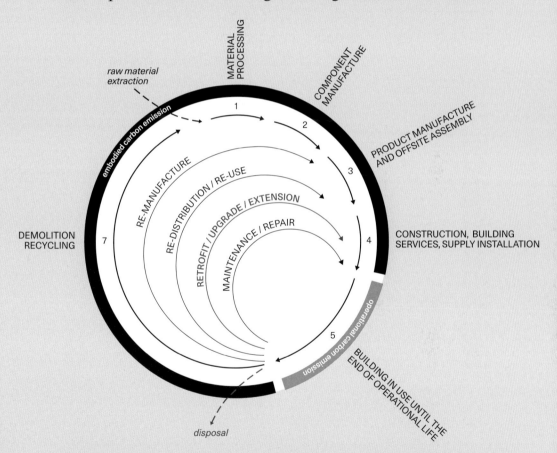

Figure 4a_ The closed loop resource model illustrates the circular economy in the construction sector as a new element necessary for the transition towards a net zero carbon emission economy. The progressive phases are indicated within a 'Whole Life Cycle Carbon Assessment' of the building and its use throughout its life, including demolition and disposal. In this context, the various reuse and life cycle extension strategies become pillars on which to build a transition from the linear economy to the circular economy, while at the same time reducing the buildings' carbon emissions. The figure shows, in particular, retrofit/upgrade/extension strategies pursued by current international legislation and regulations as a form of sustainable urban development.

most obvious choice. Adaptive reuse of existing buildings through urban redevelopment and extension programs is therefore an avenue that will be increasingly enacted and supported by community policies. Failure to pursue this scenario could result in the underestimation of the potential represented by the exploitation of the residual life expectancy of a considerable part of the buildings. Nevertheless, the concept of adaptive reuse brings with it some potential obstacles represented by the costs and the management of complex processes that stand outside the ordinary protocols of the construction sector. Moreover, in the case of vertical extensions, the constructive and structural

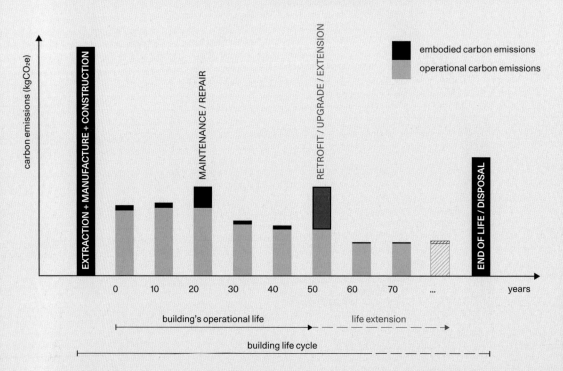

Figure 4b_ This figure shows a strategy designed to prolong the life cycle of real estate through retrofit/upgrade/extension.
In addition to ordinary maintenance and repair of existing buildings, planned interventions to most effectively reduce operational carbon emissions and, more generally, to reduce the impact of the construction industry in terms of embodied carbon emissions will become increasingly important.
[Graphics adapted from The Carbon Footprint of Construction by ACAN-Architects Climate Action Network, 2021]

implications are greater if compared with other less complex redevelopment projects. Additional loads on the buildings can require consolidation of structural elements, and surveys of the reserve structural capacity of the existing building could influence decisions regarding the most appropriate construction techniques capable of positively affecting the schedule and cost of construction and the environmental effects. So, the legitimate question is where the threshold of acceptable costs lies, beyond which this practice is not feasible, and which processes should be enacted when organizing a redevelopment project.

In the light of the various experiences in Europe, vertical extension represents a strategy of considerable interest for the market because these scenarios instantly produce a new area of commercial value, which partly compensates the cost of the retrofit, in addition to representing a practice through which it is possible to undertake complex refurbishments inside the apartments and temporarily relocate the residents to the upper story. There is also an important economic benefit, since the value of the building increases when new collective services are installed.

Obviously, in order to be able to evaluate these interventions, it is necessary to equip the construction sector with new cost-benefit analysis tools, since in some cases the benefits are of an environmental nature and cannot be calculated in monetary terms, even though they will be encouraged by the market in the future. The performance reduction of buildings during their life cycle inevitably leads to maintenance above and beyond the logic of ordinary management, which is not yet directed at systematic investments to extend the life cycle of real estate assets. Additionally, there are the technological and organizational aspects of the process, which are feasible nowadays thanks to advances in the technological innovation of the sector and in the last decade have encouraged integrated planning using off-site processes.

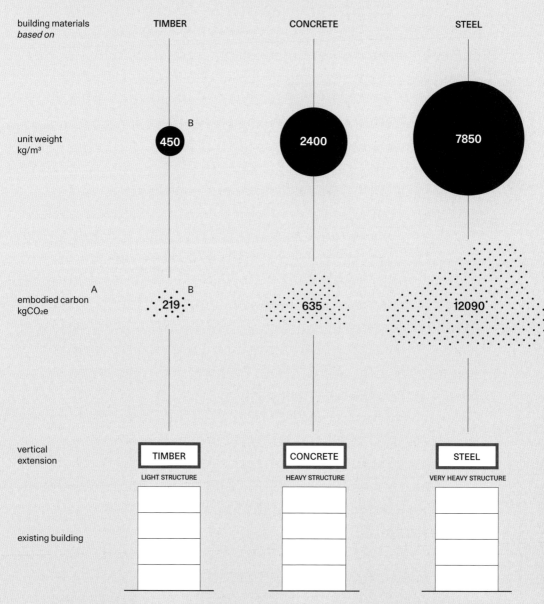

Figure 5_ Various approaches to the construction of a vertical extension. Comparison between the three building materials based on timber, concrete, and steel used in the construction systems, their unit weights, relative embodied carbon emissions, and total weight of an equivalent (for gross floor area) vertical extension.
[A: https://circularecology.com/embodied-carbon-footprint-database.html. B: values refer to CLT solid panel]

Using industrialized construction methods, adopting dry layered technologies and lightweight structural components in vertical extension projects constitute an innovative approach that supports and simplifies the redevelopment activities. The construction systems generally used for vertical extensions comprise industrialized steel and wood components. In many cases, the project is conceived on the basis of industrialized construction standards (modular design, dry assembly, scalable solutions, customization, IOT integration for predictive monitoring, etc.) and is designed to be built in the factory, dismantled and transported to the site for assembly. The organization of the process foresees greater control of the schedule and costs on site, transferring a significant part of the activity to a plant where the components are produced in the form of two- or three-dimensional cells with which to build the vertical expansions. The refurbishment of the existing structure, from the installation of new staircases and the construction of new multifunctional walls, is also undertaken in a similar manner. The off-site approach guarantees monitoring of the process in the various phases, increased quality and safety in the workplace, control of costs, and a reliable forecast of the environmental impact of the process. Apart from the speed with which the components are produced, these processes are known for the speed of execution, which can guarantee further benefits from the economic standpoint and the widespread scalability of processes.

This model also offers social benefits resulting from the organization of a construction site in a residential building, reducing disturbances, increasing workplace safety, and improving environmental factors thanks to more closely monitored production cycles and industrial processes, with a reduction of the materials needed and the waste produced, an increase in recycling during the production process and towards the end of its life, and the possibility to use bio-based materials, including engineered components.

Obviously, the prospect of reuse and vertical extension is not restricted to residential buildings; it represents seventy-five per cent of the total European real estate, but, as clearly shown by the gallery of case studies presented in this book, it also involves cultural, educational, and health activities.

An important topic dealt with in the research *Adaptive Reuse of Office Buildings: Opportunities and Risks of Conversion into Housing* by H. Remøy and T. van der Voordt[14], is represented by the conversion of under-used offices into housing, repurposing vacant buildings in the tertiary sector, the result of an unprecedented situation in Europe, USA, Japan, and Australia, a situation that has certainly been amplified by the Covid-19 emergency, with an increase in smart working policies, which will determine new markets and fields of experimentation.

The various drivers for the development of adaptive reuse will contribute, in the coming years, to amplifying the models experimented so far for the reuse of existing real estate, expanding the evaluation processes and methods to be pursued in the vision of the sustainable city, which cannot be utopic but must necessarily be feasible if we are to overcome the challenges posed at the international level and especially in Europe by 2050.

Certainly, we will see the cities from new viewpoints and what today is merely a roof, terrain for discussion and expansion, will become a new frontier for residential practices.

1   Rajat Agarwal, Shankar Chandrasekaran, and Mukund Sridhar, *Imagining construction's digital future* (McKinsey & Company, June 2016), https://www.mckinsey.com/business-functions/operations/our-insights/imagining-constructions-digital-future, accessed April 14, 2021.

2   Ignacio Zabalza Bribián, Antonio Valero Capilla, and Alfonso Aranda Usón, "Life cycle assessment of building materials: Comparative analysis of energy and environmental impacts and evaluation of the eco-efficiency improvement potential", *Building and Environment* 46, no. 5 (2011): 1133–40, https://doi.org/10.1016/j.buildenv.2010.12.002, accessed April 14, 2021.

3   Lone Feifer, *Sustainability Indicators in Buildings, Identifying Key Performance Indicators* (Lovain: Presses universitaires de Lovain, 2011), 133–39.

4   Bogdan Atanasiu, Chantal Despret, Marina Economidou, Joana Maio, Ingeborg Nolte, Oliver Rapf, Jens Laustsen, Paul Ruyssevelt, Dan Staniaszek, David Strong, and Silvia Zinetti, *Europe's Buildings Under the Microscope. A country-by-country review of the energy performance of buildings*, (Brussel: Buildings Performance Institute Europe, 2011), 7–11.

5   Hassan Abbas M. and Lee Hyowon, "The paradox of the sustainable city: definitions and examples", *Environment, development and sustainability* 17, no. 6 (December 2015): 1267–85, https://doi.org/10.1007/s10668-014-9604-z, accessed April 14, 2021.

6   About the *règles de construction d'extension vers le haut* of the city of Paris: https://api-site.paris.fr/images/85422, accessed April 14, 2021.

7   Apur, *Construire mieux et plus durable: Incidence de la loi ALUR sur l'évolution du bâti parisien*, https://www.apur.org/sites/default/files/documents/incidences_evolution_loi_ALUR_bati_parisien.pdf, accessed April 14, 2021.

8   "Town and Country Planning Regulations 2020: RPC Opinion", https://www.gov.uk/government/publications/town-and-country-planning-regulations-2020-rpc-opinion--2, accessed April 14, 2021.

9   Joan Artés, Gerardo Wadel, and Núria Martí, "Vertical Extension and Improving of Existing Buildings", *The Open Construction & Building Technology Journal* 11 (2017): 83–94, http://dx.doi.org/10.2174/1874836801711010083, accessed April 14, 2021.

10 About the SOLTAG project, which is funded under the EU's Sixth Framework Programme: https://www.buildup.eu/en/practices/cases/soltag, accessed April 14, 2021.

11 Roberto Di Giulio, "Sustainable roof-top extension: a pilot project in Florence (Italy)", in *Sustainable Building Affordable to All*, 255–63, Atti del Convegno Internazionale "Portugal SB10 - Sustainable Building Affordable to All", (Vilamoura, Algarve: Ed. University of Minho, 2010), 255–63.

12 About the REHA programme coordinated by Plan Urbanisme Construction Architecture (PUCA), a research and experiment institution of the Ministère De La Transition Ecologique et Solidaire and the Ministère De La Cohésion des Territoires et des Relations avec les Collectivités Territoriales: http://www.urbanisme-puca.gouv.fr/reha-la-rehabilitation-lourde-des-logements-un-r73.html, accessed April 14, 2021.

13 About the REHA programme calls for proposals – sessions 1, 2 and 3: http://www.urbanisme-puca.gouv.fr/appels-a-propositions-r124.html, accessed April 14, 2021.

14 Theo J M van der Voordt and Hilde Remøy, "Adaptive reuse of office buildings into housing: Opportunities and risks", *Building Research and Information: the international journal of research, development and demonstration* 42, no. 3 (2014): 381–90, https://doi.org/10.1080/09613218.2014.865922, accessed April 14, 2021.

Section II
24 Case studies

Location: Copenhagen, Denmark
Study and completion: 2004, 2011
Construction costs: 950,000 €
New floor area: 900 m² (apartments & terraces)
Architects: PLOT, JDS, BIG, EKJ
Creative authorship: Julien De Smedt, Bjarke Ingels
Project leader: Jeppe Ecklon
Client: A/B Birkegade
Photographer: JDS

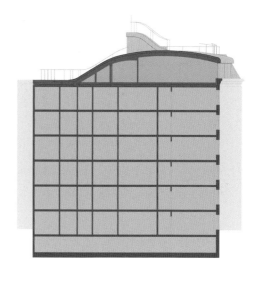

Copenhagen
01 Birkegade Rooftop Penthouses
Architects: PLOT, JDS, BIG, EKJ

The intervention has been carried out by a cooperative housing association in Birkegade, in the heart of the Nørrebro district: three new penthouse apartments and a rooftop garden were built on top of a six-story building, dating from the end of the nineteenth century. Inside the dense block of buildings there was a small and dark common courtyard: in order to remedy the lack of a livable outdoor area for the residents, the designers created a new garden on top of the housing block, giving all residents access to a wide and sunny open-air space. The garden is conceived to host different functions, each of them characterized by the association with a specific material: a children's play area with shock-absorbing orange surface, a green slope accommodating various uses, a viewing platform offering spectacular views over the city, an outdoor kitchen with barbecue area and a shielded wooden deck.

A new lightweight structure was designed to avoid excessive reliance on the existing one: the use of steel and timber trusses and horizontal plate structures in the roof and floor slabs made it possible not to position the walls of the additional story directly in correspondence with the ones below. Almost all the interior walls of the extension are made using timber studs due to their lightness.

The silhouette of the roof is punctuated by the green hill and by the two emerging stairwells: these wavy and colored shapes add a playful feeling to the space. The aim is to optimize and fully exploit the opportunities offered by the elevated position to create a usable roof garden for the occupants and an intriguing roofscape for the neighbors.

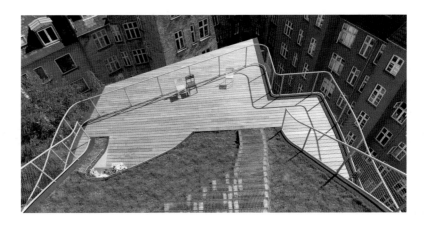

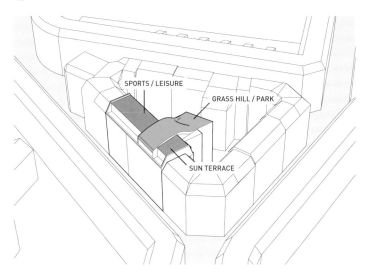

SPORTS / LEISURE

GRASS HILL / PARK

SUN TERRACE

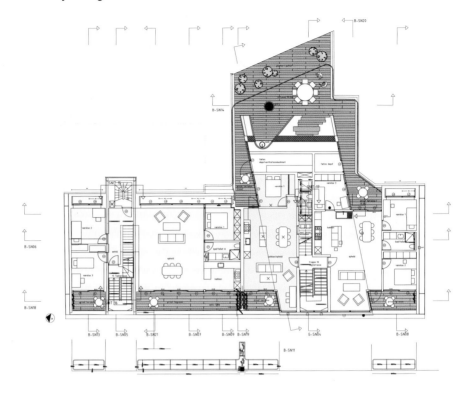

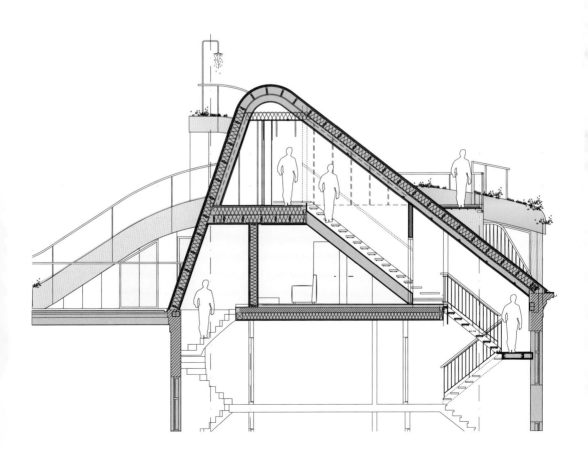

Location: Mexico City, Mexico
Completion: 2015
Gross floor area: 2,200 m²
Architects: Eduardo Cadaval & Clara Solà-Morales
Client/Real estate concept: ReUrbano
Structural engineering: Ricardo Camacho
Photographer: Miguel de Guzmán,
www.imagensubliminal.com

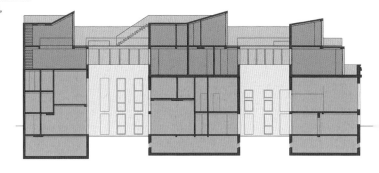

Mexico City
02 Cordoba-ReUrbano Housing
Architects: Cadaval & Solà-Morales

The building was an abandoned old house of historical value located in the Colonia Roma, a historic neighborhood in the center of Mexico City. The project is based on the initiative of the *Urban Recycling* start-up: to build housing on top of a listed building of historical value, without any parking area and incorporating a commercial part on the main floor. Nine apartments of various sizes and configurations are envisaged. The project maintains almost the entire existing building, thereby respecting the requirements set by the local monument preservation authority, establishing that only the façade was to be preserved. It is based on a detailed analysis of each of the existing elements, aiming to generate a different reality, which is, however, in harmony with the original building: past and present coexist, respecting each other and creating a new reality composed of two architectural typologies that respond to two different historical moments. The layout is structured by an external lateral corridor; the existing courtyard, which provides access to the original house, is replicated at the rear, so that the two main access cores to the units are now connected to each one of these patios.

The project grows in height, by adding intermediate levels within the existing building and two new floors on the top. To emphasize horizontality, to reduce the weight of the newly added floors, and to differentiate the original building from the new intervention, the façade of the first floor added on top of the existing building is fully glazed. A sequence of terraces and volumes changes the perception of the overall building height and makes the project more slender; it thus appears like a series of small towers and not as a continuous structure. The volumes on the upper level have their own identity, created both by the material and by the color – black, not white – to help give the roof extension a lighter appearance. The materials enhance the generation of unique spaces inside the old and the new structure, ready to be appropriated by individual and different lifestyles.

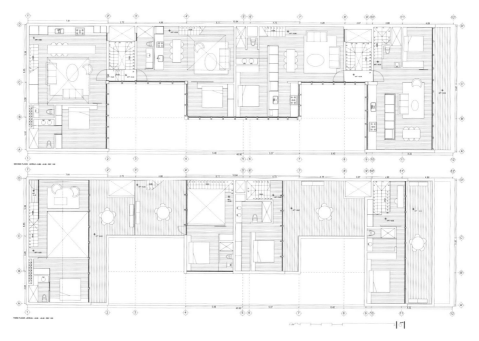

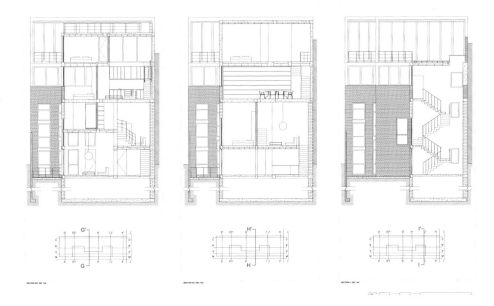

Location: Bradford, United Kingdom
Completion: 2008
Construction costs: 1,600,000 €
Gross floor area: 1,300 m²
Architects: Kraus Schönberg Architects
Client: Garbe Group
Structural engineering: EDA
Project management: Maber
Photographer: Kraus Schönberg Architects

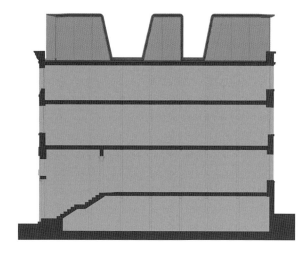

Bradford
03 Hanover House
Architects: Kraus Schönberg Architects

The development of the grade II listed Hanover House involves the refurbishment and roof extension of a Victorian warehouse building. Hanover House is located in Little Germany, a conservation area of great historical interest and beauty, in the town of Bradford. The unique character of the area is created by the uniformity of buildings, which date from the nineteenth century.

The used sandstone material and the ornamental treatment of the façades unify the blocks – although, as in many other semi-industrial areas from the period, the buildings vary in size and form and the roofscape is one of great diversity. This inspires the design of the new roof, which reinterprets the surrounding forms, sizes, and orientations.

The sculptural aspect of the roof silhouette is no mere architectural fancy, but reflects the construction of the primary structure, as well as the daylight direction and views. Aiming to create a highly efficient structure, the roof has been designed as a self-supporting system to avoid additional loading onto the existing floors. The deep floor plan of 15m required a structural solution to avoid an inefficient roof structure with oversized beams. The roof surface therefore folds up and down to a folded plate creating an engineered timber self-supporting structure, which bears on the external walls. At high level, the load bearing points of the roof are taken further into the building in order to shorten the span of the structure from 15m to 10m. The inclined balcony side walls transfer the reaction forces at these points into the external wall. Any resulting lateral force is transferred into the floor plate which acts as a tie. The roof surface is made of cross-laminated engineered timber boards. The 140mm thick board has a good U-value and adds up to a highly insulated roof.

The chosen roof cladding re-interprets the traditional slate tiled roofs of the neighborhood with a modern material. Similar in appearance the new roof is clad in anthracite pre-patinated standing seam zinc. The complex roof geometry with various ridges and valleys, inclined walls, folds, bends and radiused corners required a construction technique which could accommodate these conditions. The standing seam zinc roof was an optimal solution for this challenge. The spatial concept has merged with the construction and structure, forming one entity.

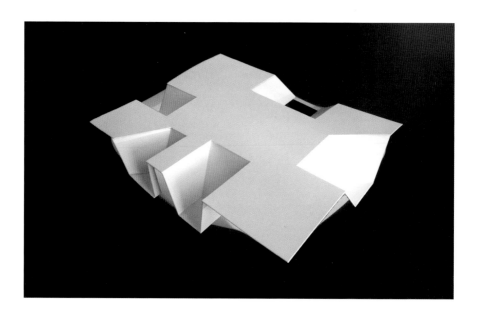

Location: Vienna, Austria
Study and completion: 2006, 2012
Construction costs: 3,600,000 €
New floor area: 1,290 m²
Architects: Josef Weichenberger architects + Partner
Client: K&TF Immobilien GmbH & Co KG
Structural engineering: KS Ingenieure ZT GmbH
Building physics: Dipl.-Ing. Erich Röhrer Staatl. Bef. und Beeid. ZT für Bauwesen
Construction supervision: Bauconsult Bau- und Planungsgesellschaft m.b.H.
HVAC engineering: ZFG Projekt- und Planungs GmbH
Electrical engineering: TB Eipeldauer + Partner GmbH
Photographer: Erika Mayer

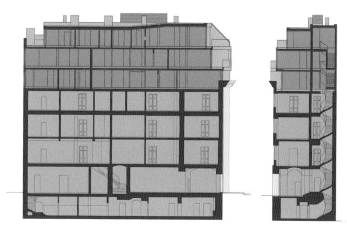

Vienna
04 Margaretenstrasse 9
Architects: Josef Weichenberger architects + Partner

The project is an example of sculptural integration into the historical urban fabric. The architect responded to the demands of the client – maximum floor area, striking views and terraces, compliance with building codes – by creating a morphologically complex project. The building is situated in a conservation zone, so the design process was carried out in dialogue with the building authorities and the design advisory committee.

The sloping profile of the traditional roof was respected by arranging the three new levels in a gradually receding formation, creating a skyline of terraced vertical façades: the new floors appear as staggered and overlapping ribbon-like volumes, shaped according to the geometric reference derived from the directions of the irregular five-street intersection.

The rooms are laid out along the façades and separated by sliding doors with a second internal opening: these transverse walls allow individual areas to be combined or separated as desired. Despite the building's relatively small footprint, it was possible to create terraces by staggering the volumes. Continuous glazing installed using dark gray metal profiles, with an integrated exterior sunshade system, clearly contrast with the historical house below, providing a new inhabited roof.

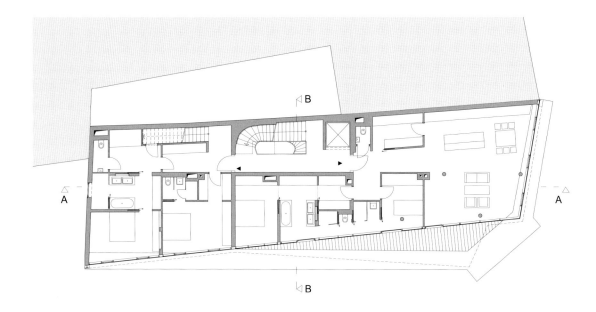

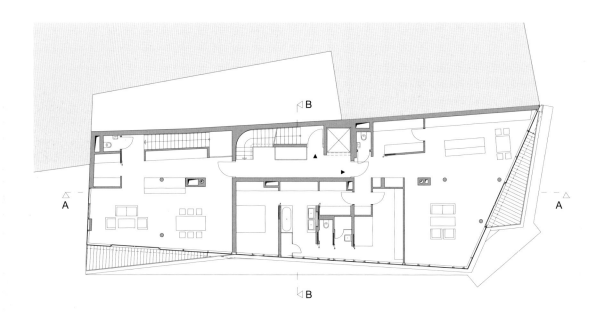

Location: Barcelona, Spain
Completion: 2008
Gross floor area: 2,500 m^2
Architects: Octavio Mestre + Costaserra Arquitectura
Client: ARESA (Mutua Madrileña)
Structural engineering: Eskubi SL
Building physics: Promec
Photographer: Lluis Casals

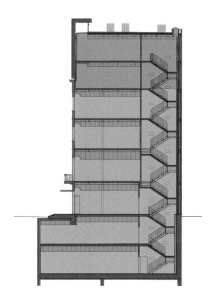

Barcelona
05 Aresa Clinic
Architects: Octavio Mestre + Costaserra Arquitectura

The building of the old Olivé Gumà Clinic is located at the edge of the urban extension based on the Cerdà plan and was listed as historical. The need to convert and expand the clinic led the architects to rebuild the existing floors, preserving the façades, and to add two new levels reaching the height of the nearby buildings. The floors are built with a lightweight structure of interacting slabs and metal pillars. The new volumes are designed as a forceful sculptural intervention that escapes an imitating attitude: the extension consists of a glazed volume protected by a corten steel structure that acts as a sunshade and at the same time creates a dense, rhythmic façade. The outer skin is made up of L-shaped elements composed of 8mm thick weathering steel plates, assembled one by one on site. The same material is used for the window modules on the façade, which are made of extruded corten steel boxes that are reminiscent of the new addition and distinguish the character of the building.

The interior façade consists of aluminum elements with thermal break and laminated glass: contact between this recessed transparent inner skin and the new envelope is achieved by means of a curved section that almost disappears in the shadows of the vertical steel plates. The contemporary volume enters into a dialogue with the old building through a simple language of clean lines.

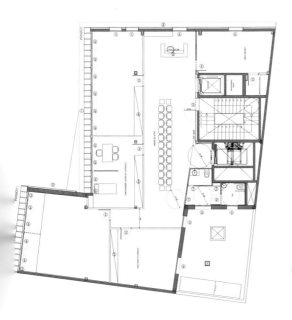

Location: Vienna, Austria
Study and completion: 2008/2010, 2012
Construction costs: 1,000,000 €
New floor area: 526 m^2 (apartment & terraces)
Architects: PPAG architects
Client: Baugruppe Radetzkystrasse
Structural engineering: werkraum
Building physics: Bauklimatik
Building services engineering: Bauklimatik
Shell and timber construction: D&K - Dach und Bau
Extension and construction work: A&H Bau GmbH
Photographer: Roland Krauss

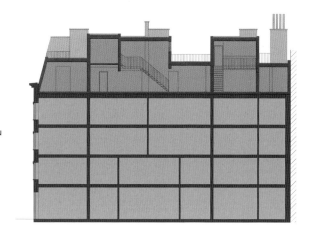

Vienna
06 Radetzkystrasse 6
Architects: PPAG architects

The project is an example of an inner-city re-densification process: the attic space of a typical nineteenth-century building was used as an elevated construction site for a new residential complex with several units. Around a small raised plaza, accessible by an elevator, slightly receding cubic structures are arranged. The apartments are a sequence of differently proportioned rooms with varying ceiling heights, resulting from a careful handling of the strict legal framework conditions. They are built using a low-energy timber frame construction.

Each apartment consists of room cubes of varying size and height, all with a unique character. The room proportions correspond to the individual uses. Window openings facing in all directions capture the daylight, and a homogenous layer of plaster adds a finish to the highly individualized interior. While some of the cubes feature a gallery level, others extend over two floors (connected by an internal staircase) or just have one single floor. Accordingly, room heights vary from a minimum of 2.30 meters to a maximum of 5.00 meters, resulting in a vivid roofscape that recalls the image of a village. At the same time, due to their uniform surface, the resultant almost homogenous appearance respects the conservation area regulations.

Location: Seoul, South Korea
Completion: 2014
New floor area: 350 m²
Architects: Design Guild
Photographer: Design Guild

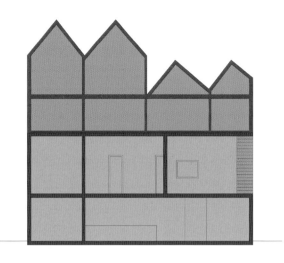

Seoul
07 Loft House "The black"
Architects: Design Guild

The project is located in a residential district of Seoul, made up of ordinary detached building types and narrow streets. According to the designers' intention, the project should act as a transformative force in the dull urban landscape, providing unusual shapes that would attract people, while maintaining the harmony and balance between old and new. A low detached house was renovated and expanded in order to create a guest house. To bear the load of the vertical extension, a new steel structure and another floor slab were superimposed onto the existing building. Four volumes with gabled roofs were built on top of this base, each with a different height. All the units have their own attic that is accessible via an internal staircase; all have a different design to mark their individuality. For the new addition, a lightweight wooden construction was used to reduce the overall load.

The steel columns and beams at the front side support the vertical extension and provide common balconies. To soften the visual autonomy of the four volumes, the exterior walls are plastered and painted in dark gray and punctuated with white window frames: this continuous exterior skin makes the façades appear as if carved from a unique raw material. The different dimension of the volumes and the irregular rhythm of the openings create a diverse appearance but, at the same time, a homogeneous and coherent one.

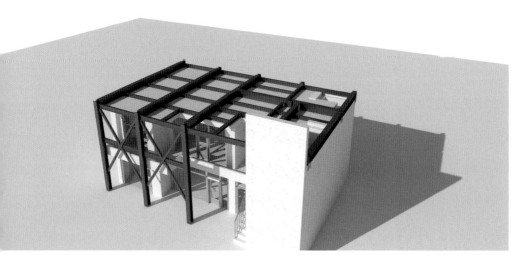

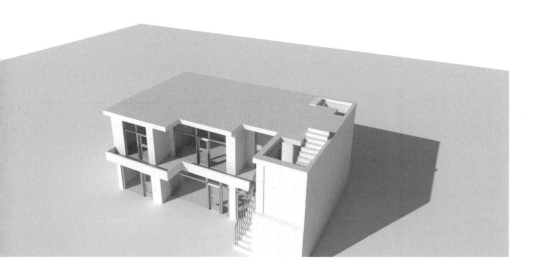

Location: Cehegín, Spain
Study and completion: 2007, 2010
Construction costs: 115,000 €
New floor area: 224 m^2 (apartment & terraces)
Architects: GRUPO ARANEA
Client: LUDE (Juan Antonio Ludeña)
Photographer: Jesús Granada

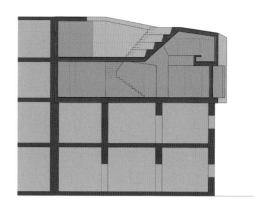

Cehegín
08 Casa Lude
Architects: Grupo Aranea

The building is located in the dense urban fabric of the village of Cehegín. The project sought to achieve a visual balance of solids and voids, within which the giant windows are holes that do not directly face the street and the neighboring houses, in order to safeguard the privacy of the users, but afford views of the surrounding landscape: Casa Lude thus reinterprets the massiveness and introversion of the traditional architecture in the area. Thick walls, little glass and the white color protect from the heat of southern Spain.

The new structure is connected to the original house using the existing stairwell. Within the sculptural volume of the extension, the space is modeled in a three-dimensional way: flowing spaces, defined by light, intertwine at different levels, both internally and externally, and extend to the rooftop as a natural continuation of the interior life.

The two sections – old and new – express a sort of symbiotic relationship. Towards the top, the house appears as a massive excavated volume, arranged according to the needs of the interior space, which becomes more introspective and seems to be defined by the light that passes through.

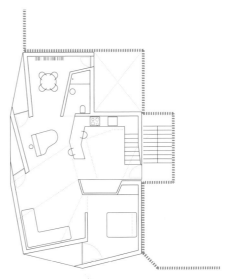

FIRST FLOOR

0 1 2 3   5 m

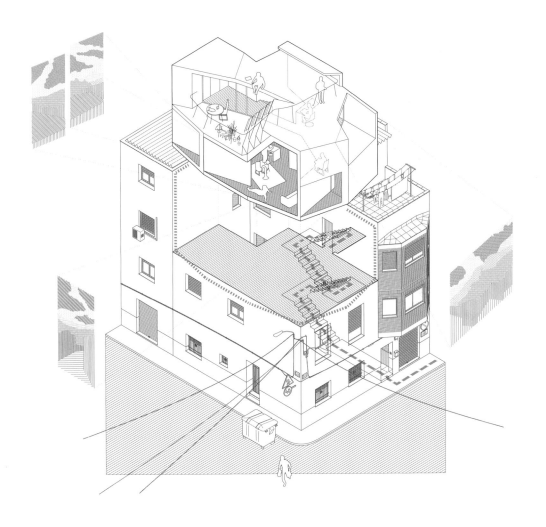

Location: Paris, France
Study and completion: 2006, 2012
Construction costs: 9,100,000 €
New floor area: 1,808 m²
Architects: Atelier d'Architecture Marie
Schweitzer
Client: Pax-Progrès-Pallas of the
Domaxis Group
Tenant/operator: Coallia
Photographer: Atelier d'Architecture Marie
Schweitzer

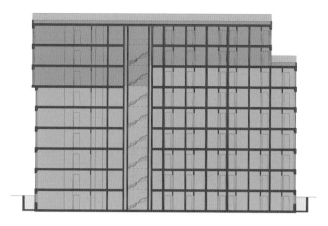

Paris
09 Tolbiac Housing Rehabilitation
Architects: Atelier d'Architecture Marie Schweitzer

The task was the rehabilitation and extension of the Coallia migrant workers' residence located on Rue de Tolbiac, in the 13th district. The existing building from the nineteen-seventies was designed by architect Jean Puttati. It is composed of two blocks of four and five levels with a square plan.

The addition of two and three floors respectively allowed the creation of 70 new rooms. The new façades are finished with a natural larch wood cladding. The floors and the roof are built of prefabricated elements made of screwed spruce slats, left visible inside the building.

This wooden vertical extension represents a relevant densification strategy for an existing building, trying to meet the requirements of the client and urban regulations. The speed of installing the wooden elements (one week for assembling a 400m² floor area) facilitated re-housing during construction. The need to build the new part in a short time and with little load (the three wooden floors weigh as much as one floor in reinforced concrete) led the designers to experiment with environmentally friendly technologies together with the municipality and other stakeholders involved.

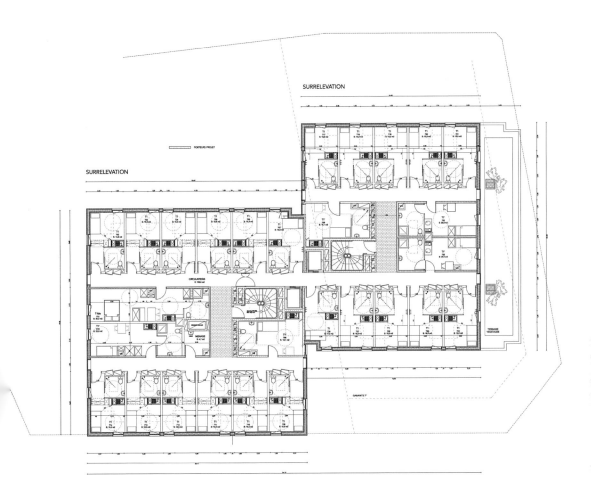

Location: Cinisello Balsamo, Milano, Italy
Completion: 2007
New floor area: 1,420 m²
Architects: studio Albori (Emanuele Almagioni, Giacomo
Borella, Francesca Riva)
Client: Comune di Cinisello Balsamo
Structural engineering: FVprogetti
Building physics: studio Barrese
Photographer: studio Albori

Milano
10 Cinisello Balsamo Social Housing Complex
Architects: studio Albori

The project extends two social housing complexes built in the nineteen-eighties, exploiting the regional law on the "conversion of attics for residential use." Once the pitched roof in sheet metal was demolished, a series of terraced houses and a small building for communal use were realized on top of the eighth floor. Access was provided via a covered porch.

The new townhouses are built in wood, iron, and aluminum. The green roofs ensure good thermal insulation and provide a garden for each residential unit.

The access routes, the "small villa" for common use and its garden, the lawns on the rooftops, and the small buildings that occupy them (which serve as a tool shed/boiler room; in the project equipped with solar thermal panels) form a sort of hanging urban micro-environment, with panoramic views of Milan and the distant mountains.

Problems due to disputes with the construction company, which abandoned the building site, caused a delay in the completion and technical defects. Nevertheless, the civic spirit and the inventiveness of the inhabitants have transformed the spaces – by planting the roof gardens (left bare by the contractor) and adding pergolas, tables, barbecues –, making the roofscape a vibrant populated place.

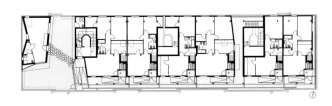

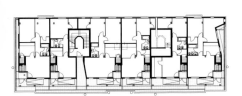

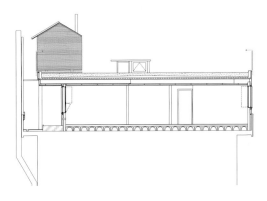

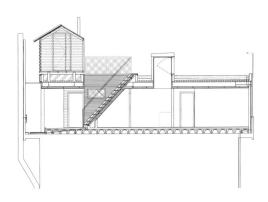

Location: Cologne, Germany
Completion: 2010
Construction costs: 26,995,000 €
Gross floor area: 25,600 m²
Architects: Archplan GbR
Client: LEG Wohnen NRW GmbH
Structural engineering/building physics/quality
assurance management: Archplan GbR
Photographer: Archplan GbR

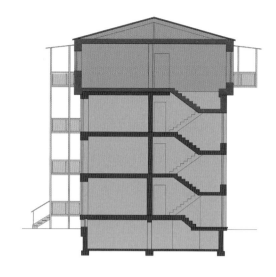

Cologne
11   Ford Estate of LEG
Architects: Archplan

The existing estate was built in the early nineteen-fifties as workers' dwellings for the Ford factory and comprised 11 blocks with a total of 300 residential units. The flats had an average floor area of 47 square meters each and were heated with coal-burning stoves; only a few had small balconies, and the sanitary and electric installations were obsolete. The main goals of the intervention were: conversion of small flats into family flats by merging three into two units, provision of balconies, renewal of the technical installations including all bathrooms, improvement of open spaces with kitchen gardens, playgrounds and meeting points. To boost the real estate value, the area had to be upgraded to maximum housing space: one new level, and in certain areas a second one, were added to the three-story buildings. More than 6,300 square meters (81 new flats) were added to the existing 14,200 square meters. A cross-laminated timber construction was put over the top floor, which was not capable of bearing an additional load. The frame construction was delivered including the windows, the finished surface on the inside, and the first two layers of plaster on the outside. It was supplied with a maximum length of 12 meters. The whole structure for an 80-meter block of flats took about one week to be erected, from the deconstruction of the roof to the completion of the timber frame; the construction of the new story was independent from the renovation of the existing flats. A 45-centimeter protrusion distinguishes the new level, painted in vivid Mediterranean colors, from the renovated existing ones. In terms of energy conservation, significant results have been achieved: highly efficient insulation of external walls, basement, and top floor ceilings; new windows and doors with heat-absorbing glazing; air ventilation systems for each flat, with heat recovery in the top floor flats; heating and hot water supply by gas condensing boiler technology and solar panels.

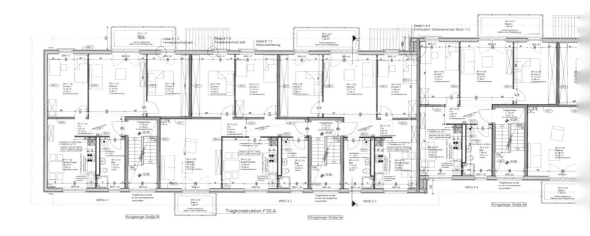

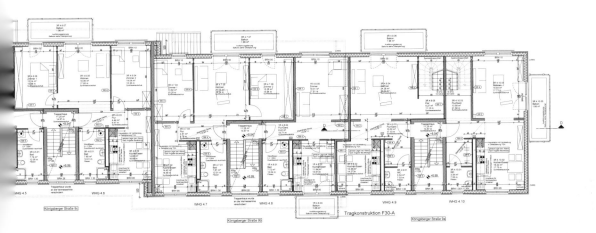

Location: Stockholm, Sweden
Completion: 2003
Gross floor area: 6,500 m²
Architects: Equator Stockholm AB
Client: Fastighets AB Certus
Photographer: Equator Stockholm AB

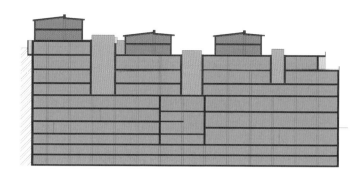

Stockholm
12 Klara Zenit Roofscape
Architects: Equator Stockholm AB

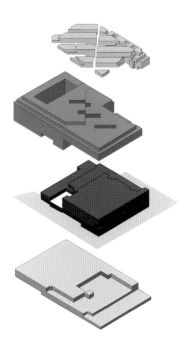

Klara Zenit reflects the political ambition of reclaiming the center of Stockholm for housing. For many years, the central area of the city had been turned into a business district, where apartments had successively been replaced by offices.

When the block was purchased from the postal administration with the intention of renovating it, the City of Stockholm indicated that part of the project had to accommodate a residential function: an agreement was signed to create 100 flats in the block as a key to the redevelopment. The challenge was how to include housing in the project without affecting the property value.

The roof constituted the new "ground" where to place the new houses, respecting the position of skylights and patios providing light for the offices below. The apartments use the diagonal direction of the existing structural grid to best support the additional loads. Thanks to the wooden construction, no reinforcement was needed for the concrete structure below the terraces.

This new village on the top has its own identity that blends into Stockholm's roofscape: it is a small community, like a village without cars, and a safe playground for kids. Over the years, the inhabitants have appropriated this exceptional location, changing the boundaries between private and common terraces, implementing new common areas for football, field hockey and barbecues like a real public park on the roof.

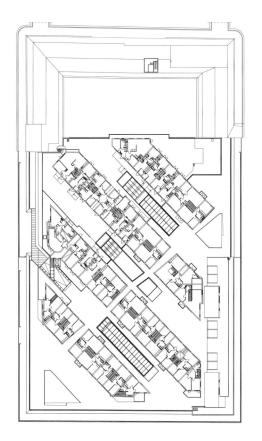

Location: Oisterwijk, the Netherlands
Completion: 2018
Gross floor area: 1,200 m^2
Architects: Wenink Holtkamp Architecten
Developer industrial heritage: BOEi
Contractor/developer: Nico de Bont TBI
Building consultation: K+
Mechanical installation: Van Thiel Optimaal
Electrical installation: Copal
Photographer: Tim van de Velde, www.tvdv.be

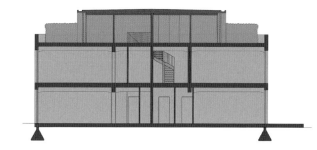

Oisterwijk
13 De Lakfabriek
Architects: Wenink Holtkamp Architecten

De Lakfabriek is an industrial building designed in 1925 by architect A. Benoit and is part of the former leather factory complex KVL, one of the largest leather producers in Europe for years. Since 2001, the plant complex has undergone a refurbishment process, which has turned it into an attractive area. De Lakfabriek is the first renovated building on the site to serve a residential purpose.

The project aimed at preserving the industrial character of the former factory and at enhancing the original carefully designed brick façades and concrete structures.

A low glazed extension has been added to the roof: the modern and minimalist structure clearly distinguishes itself from the brick building below, emphasizing it in a respectful way: this volume is recessed in relation to the existing façade, leaving space for large roof terraces.

The industrial look is maintained by using new slender aluminum window frames with a classic profile that relate to the original steel window frames, and by leaving the raw concrete structure visible wherever possible inside the twenty-five housing units. These units were conceived in three different types: studios, apartments and ground-floor flats; the layout of each house was designed in consultation with the future residents.

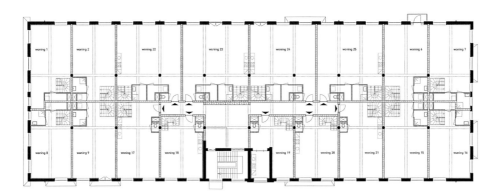

0 1 2   6m

floorplan first floor new

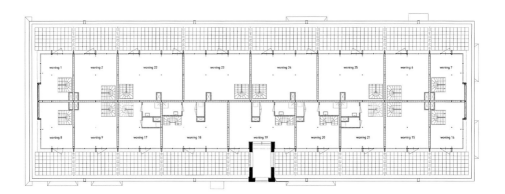

0 1 2   6m

floorplan roof exstention

Location: Antwerp, Belgium
Study and completion: 2009, 2010
Construction costs: 3,800,000 €
Architects: Stramien cvba
Client: SD Worx
Structural engineering: Arcade nv
Building physics: Cenergie cvba
Art: Benoît Van Innis
Photographer: Stramien cvba

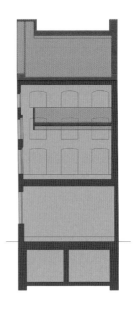

Antwerp
14 Kendall Building
Architects: Stramien cvba

A sort of long core that runs through every level of the building was installed against the wall towards the adjoining building, containing all the services. The entire floor area along this enclosed space remains open and can be used as a large and flexible office space. Artist Benoit van Innis created a design concept for the wall that extends through the entire building. This abstract pattern of lines and colors ties the levels together, while still retaining a unique character for each floor.

The existing mansard roof, a subsequent addition to the original warehouse, was not high enough; it was therefore replaced with a new transparent steel structure. The regular rhythm of this new floor matches the austere red brick of the original warehouse. The new extension visually contrasts with the existing building; but while the exterior of the building clearly differs from the new vertical extension, the compositional language and the spatial layout inside are the same, unifying the new and the old parts.

The Kendall office is located in a former warehouse in Antwerp's old dockyards. The building had undergone a range of interventions until an overall transformation turned the old warehouse into a contemporary office block. Due to the fact that the stories were not very high, and consequently quite dark, the architects decided to remove a floor slab in the middle of the building, thus providing a change in terms of layout and guaranteeing sufficient natural light for every story.

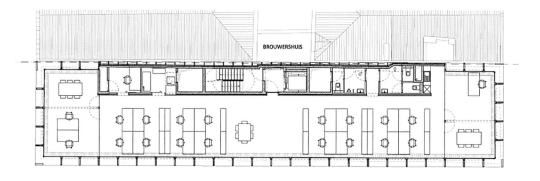

nieuwe toestand

Location: Budapest, Hungary
Study and completion: 2006, 2020
Gross floor area: 6,350 m^2
Architects: T2.a Architects
Client: MERKAPT Zrt.
Photographer: Zsolt Batár

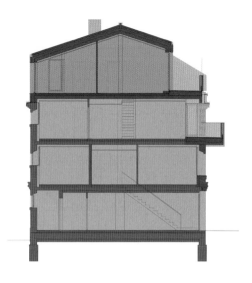

Budapest
15 Jazz Loft
Architects: T2.a Architects

The renovation of an abandoned nineteenth-century mill evolved through several changes: the works that had begun in 2005 stopped for almost a decade, then a new property owner resumed the refurbishment of the abandoned and deteriorated structures.

The mill retains its original appearance towards the street, with the exception of new fixtures and oversized openings near the stairway entrances. The new roof extension is a volume with a gray brick slip cladding that counterpoints the mass underneath, providing a new roof. The openings are larger than those below and the compositional rhythm is independent from the series of old façade pilasters. Such contrast produces a visual shift that introduces to the different shape of the interior elevation. At the rear, the lack of the original façade required a new one: a heavy material was proposed – purple clinker bricks – in order to recall the materiality of the old façade bricks, but also to create a modern appearance. The inward-facing walls – which overlook a garden area for the neighbors – have a much more playful appearance to them, as they are counterpointed by colored balcony parapets, matching the brick colors.

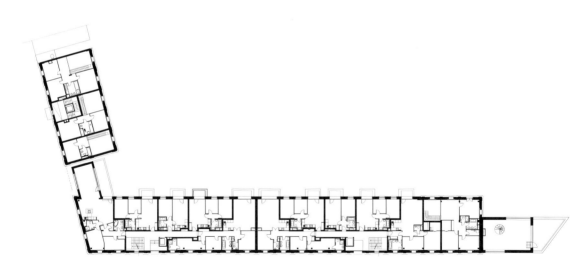

Location: Sheffield, United Kingdom
Completion: 2012
Construction costs: 1,300,000 €
Gross floor area: 810 m²
Architects: Project Orange
Client: Cristian Sinclair
Structural engineering: Project Design Associates
Project management: JP Mooney Ltd
Photographer: Jack Hobhouse

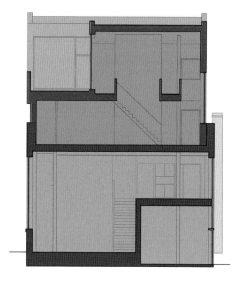

Sheffield
16 192 Shoreham Street
Architects: Project Orange

192 Shoreham Street is a former Victorian industrial brick building sited at the edge of the Cultural Industries Quarter Conservation Area of Sheffield: it was not listed but considered locally significant.

The rehabilitation of the building aimed at introducing new leisure and working activities, to be relevant in its transforming context and celebrating its industrial heritage. The brief was to provide mixed use, combining a double-height restaurant/bar within the original shell with duplex studio office units above. These units are accommodated in an upward extension of the existing building, designed as a contrasting but complementary volume, a sort of replacement for the original pitched roof. The cladding of the extension is formed from insulated panels covered with sinusoidal, powder-coated aluminum profiled sheets. The roof is finished with an extensive sedum roof. The construction consists of a lightweight steel frame with composite concrete/steel floor decks. The steel frame both supports the extension and retains the original brick walls, in dialogue with the unique raw industrial character.

The new extension is an abstract evocation of the industrial roofscapes that used to dominate this part of the city. It is complementary to the existing building: it attaches discreetly to the building section underneath thanks to a slightly recessed part, but it engages with the host structure in a couple of locations, where windows bite into it.

The new roof contour creates dramatic sweeping ceiling profiles in the new accommodation through a sectional dynamism, further enhanced by the use of double-height volumes in the duplex units created. The proposal was intended to enhance the building's identity, as a symbol both of the ancient times of that area and its ongoing transformation.

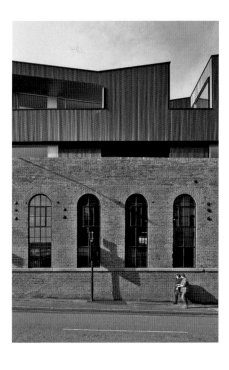

1 B1 unit
2 Void below
3 WCs
4 Circulation core
5 Lift
6 Terrace

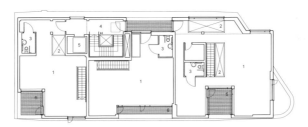

1 A3 unit
2 Kitchen
3 Bin store
4 Cycle store
5 Entrance
6 Secondary entrance
7 WCs
8 Stairs to mezzanine
9 Circulation core
10 Lift

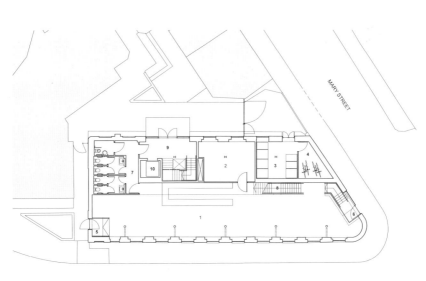

MARY STREET

SHOREHAM STREET

Location: Huangpu District, Shanghai, China
Study and completion: 2008/2010, 2010
Gross floor area: 2,800 m^2
Architects: Neri&Hu Design and
Research Office
Interior design: Neri&Hu Design and
Research Office
Owner/developer/investor: Cameron
Holdings Hotel Management Limited
Structural engineering: China Jingye
Engineering Technology Company
Building physics: Far East Consulting
Engineers Limited
Photographer: Pedro Pegenaute

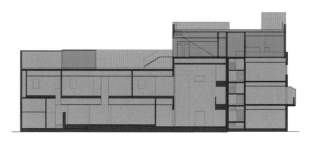

Shanghai
17 The Waterhouse at South Bund
Architects: Neri&Hu Design and Research Office

The Waterhouse Hotel is located by the new Cool Docks development in the South Bund District of Shanghai, facing the Huangpu River. The hotel is accommodated in an existing three-story building from the nineteen-thirties, which used to be a Japanese Army headquarters. The idea was to maintain the building's stripped concrete structure with brick walls and to add a new corten steel extension on the top. The original restored concrete building and its vertical extension reflect the industrial past of this working dock: the corten steel cladding of the new volume on the fourth floor evokes the industrial nature of the ships passing by on the river.

The approach of mixing new and old has been implemented for both the exterior and interior appearance. The character of the hotel showcases a sort of perceptual inversion between the inside and outside features. Almost blind external façades, with high window cut-outs, seem to express to the outside a concept of minimal intervention. By contrast, the inner courtyard is a surprisingly bright and vibrant space, with white walls punctuated with a multitude of modern flush windows.

From the inside, the private spaces invite looking out over the city and the river, as do the large vertical window above the reception desk and the corridor windows overlooking the dining room. These unexpected visual connections add an element of surprise, reminding of the narrow alleys called "longtang" of Shanghai's traditional dense urban pattern.

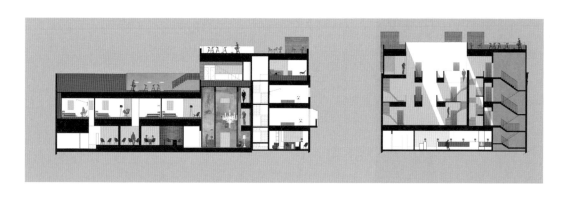

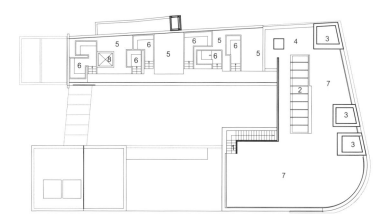

north

1 stair to roof bar
2 skylight
3 periscope
4 bar
5 sunken garden
6 seating pocket
7 seating area
8 void to guest room

Location: Tallinn, Estonia
Study and completion: 2006, 2009
Gross floor area: 9,002 m^2
Architects: HGA (Hayashi-
Grossschmidt Arhitektuur)
Client: Rotermann City
Structural engineering: Neoprojekt
Building physics: Hevac
Electrical engineering: Nord Projekt
Detailed planning: K Projekt
Project management: Projektipea
Photographers: Arne Maasik, Martin
Siplane, Sven Soome, Tomomi Hayashi

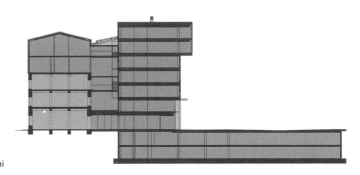

Tallinn

18 Rotermann's Old and New Flour Storage
Architects: HGA (Hayashi-Grossschmidt Arhitektuur)

The Old Flour Storage is an old limestone building dating from 1904, located in the Rotermann Quarter, a former industrial area for food production between Tallinn's old town and the port.

The project consists in the rehabilitation of the Old Flour Storage, with the addition of two stories, the construction of the New Flour Storage, and of the atrium connecting the two volumes. The ground floor is reserved for retail activities, all other levels accommodate offices. The complex was to face a plaza as a new focal point of the quarter.

The design approach aimed to refer to the identity of the old industrial quarter. The façade of the extension shows a rhythm of solids and voids that echoes the proportion of wall versus window openings of the building below. Corten steel was chosen for its property to blend into the existing surroundings with its rough surfaces: limestone walls, brick lintels, and rusted steel details. It pays homage to the area's industrial past.

The same material is used for the volume of the New Flour Storage, which contrasts the regular rhythm of the old building, displaying a sort of "communicative" façade towards the plaza. Its windows have three different sizes: the small ones are to frame the views and allow fresh air to enter, the medium-sized ones relate to the human scale, while the cantilevered larger windows are used to provide space for meeting rooms or communal areas with panoramic views of the plaza and the old town.

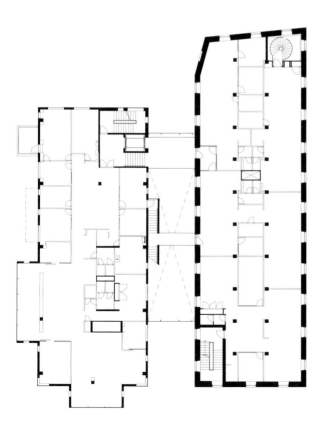

Location: Roubaix, France
Completion: 2008
Construction costs: 3,325,000 €
Gross floor area: 4,549 m²
Architects: Tank Architectes
(Olivier Camus & Lyderic Veauvy)
Client: Maison Rouar
Photographer: Jean-Pierre Duplan

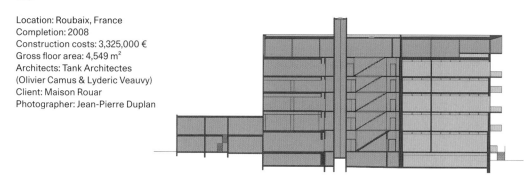

Roubaix
19 La Minoterie
Architects: Tank Architectes

The project deals with the rehabilitation of a former flour mill and an industrial building into residential units along the Roubaix canal. The nineteenth-century south wing appeared as a five-story brick "industrial castle," with the classic façades composed of vertical openings emphasized by pilasters; the adjacent wing was a six-story post-and-beam frame volume in reinforced concrete. The project envisaged the demolition of the upper level of the concrete volume in order to align it with the older part of the building.

Four penthouses were created on top, forming an asymmetrical cross placed on the existing supporting structure. Their metal frame reduces the load and provides unobstructed volumes underneath the visible steel deck, which accentuates the "loft" effect. The varied apartment sizes correspond to the solar orientation, and all apartments benefit from a corner terrace. The largest unit opens up towards the south via a loggia that spans across the old brick façade: this loggia juts out more than two meters from the old façade and has a streamlined aluminum cladding. Eight balconies of a similar scale are "hung" on the front: their opaque sides conceal the steel tie rod, while a frameless glass pane serves as a balustrade, conveying the impression of openness towards the landscape and of an architectural juxtaposition to the old brick mill. In the other part of the building, recesses were randomly placed in the enclosed volume, thus creating numerous loggias that make the concrete framework more noticeable: the concrete has been left in its raw state, so that the visible load-bearing structure adds a gray patina that corresponds to the color of the aluminum frames and parapets, emphasizing the former industrial atmosphere of the building.

Location: Frankfurt/Main, Germany
Completion: 2003
Construction costs: 890,000 €
Gross floor area: 980 m², effective area 586 m²
Architects: Index Architekten
Client: Frankfurt Office for Science and Art
Photographer: Wolfgang Günzel, Christof Lison

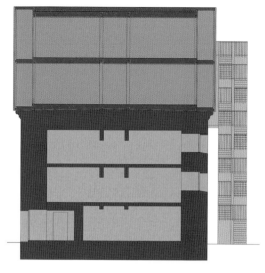

Frankfurt/Main
20 Cultural Bunker
Architects: Index Architekten

The existing building is a disused bunker built in 1940 in Frankfurt's Osthafen, masked as a house, with a hip roof to disguise it and protect against bombs. Due to the mass of the structure – the outer walls were about two meters thick – demolition would have been very expensive. The project proposed to turn the former bunker into a cultural venue providing space for artistic purposes, with the aim of promoting the renovation of this industrial area. The bunker identity was revealed by removing the elements that masked it, and in a sense the structure lent itself as an elevated construction site.
Inside the heavy concrete mass, rehearsal rooms for musicians were installed; on top of the old structure, a light timber construction was added, housing new studios and rooms for artists for the Institute of New Media. The addition is a lightweight double-story wooden box with a height of 6.40 meters, surrounded by an external corridor that is protected by a metal grid structure and aligned with the bunker's longitudinal walls: shifting the new structure off the bunker's center created a four-meter cantilever eastwards and freed space for common use on the opposite side, close to the access staircase.
The metal grid façade counterpoints the concrete walls, creating the image of a compact, light, and mobile box; from the inside, the grid provides an open view of the cityscape.

The project integrates itself into the context: it does not deny the existing identity, but it uses it as a support for the creation of new activities that can bring quality of life to this part of the city.

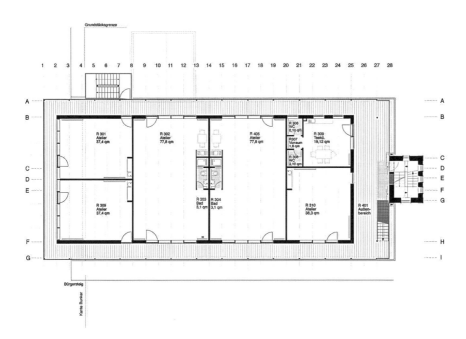

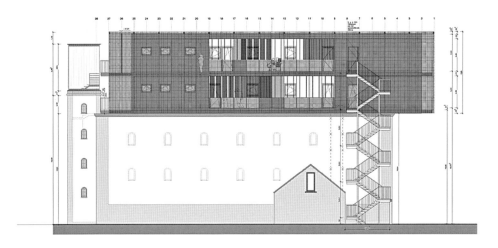

Location: Lima, Peru
Study and completion: 2007, 2012
Gross floor area: 2,280 m^2
Architects: Sandra Barclay and Jean Pierre Crousse
Client: Inversiones Alternas
Structural engineering: Zegarra-Yeckle
Building physics: Manuel Chamorro
Electricity and lighting: Diaz-Luy
Contractor: EITAL S.A.
Photographer: Elsa Ramirez, Jose Luis Dieguez,
Jean Pierre Crousse

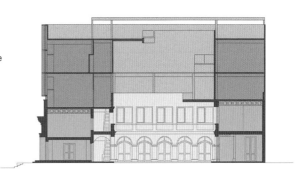

Lima
21 Visual Arts School
Architects: Barclay & Crousse Architecture

The existing building is a remarkable example of neo-colonial architecture of the nineteen-thirties. The renovation and extension project for the Visual Arts School of Lima had to respectfully deal with the existing building in order to give shape to a new complex that is an expression of contemporariness.

One of the challenges was the simultaneous use of two different building techniques: the adobe and traditional masonry of the old building, on which the new stories were to be placed, and the independent and very light extension structure itself. The use of a prefabricated steel structure allowed an easy intervention on top of the existing building and a fast execution, so that the school could recommence activities in a very short time. The merging of traditional and new spaces was achieved around the patio. This traditional open place is the core of the building: the project extends the void upwards, intersecting it with open skywalks that link existing staircases to comply with fire regulations. These open skywalks have steel grid floors, so natural light can easily get through to the ground floor, creating a new open space where students from different disciplines can meet each other.

Tradition and modernity are clearly visible from the street: tradition – the opaque existing building – is the base for the new, seemingly weightless and transparent addition, both literally and figuratively. The new exterior façade recalls kinetic art, as the shading elements seem to change their color as the viewer moves down the street. In the interior, the steel skywalks form a photographic diaphragm when seen from the entrance patio, a tribute to one of the disciplines that the extension will bring to the school.

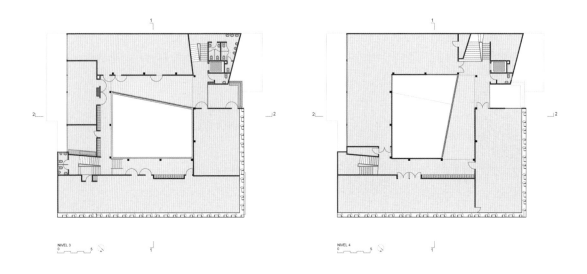

NIVEL 3
0   5

NIVEL 4
0   5

Location: Valparaíso, Chile
Completion: 2014
Gross floor area: 985 m²
Architect: Joaquín Velasco Rubio
Client: Inmobiliaria Meli Ltda
Engineering: Luis Della Valle Solari
Photographer: Aryeh Kornfeld

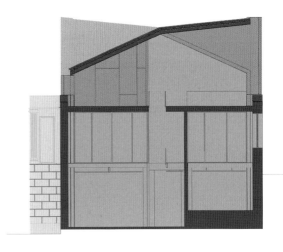

Valparaíso
22 Dinamarca 399
Architect: Joaquín Velasco Rubio

The renovation of an early twentieth-century building – the former residence of the Consul of Denmark – was aimed at the construction of a multicultural center for cultural activities and artistic events, as well as for collaborative workspaces with meeting room, cafeteria, and restaurant.

The project is based on a respectful dialogue between tradition and technology: the contemporary intervention was implemented as a metal structure on the existing reinforced concrete building, generating flexible and luminous spaces inside. The history of the building and its material decay was deliberately left exposed: as a result, the structure still appears to be unfinished.

The new volume blends gently into the historical building, thanks to the use of large windows with corten frames. In the interior, the new additions, such as stairs or partitions, are made of steel. The architectural composition of the new volume is independent of the one below. Yet, the two buildings dialogue harmoniously through the slenderness of the rigid lines and the transparency created by the large openings of the new part.

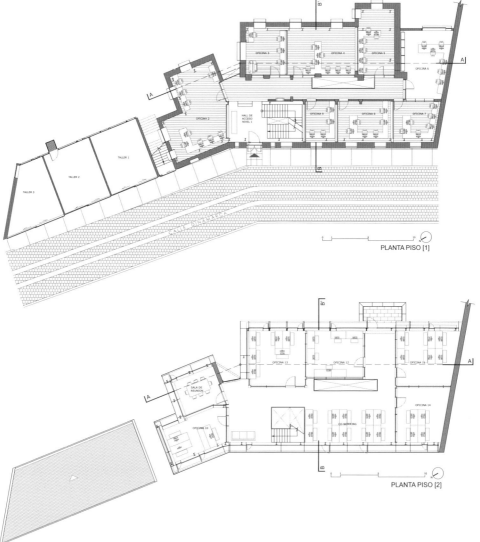

PLANTA PISO [1]

PLANTA PISO [2]

Location: Berlin, Germany
Study and completion: 2014, 2020
Gross floor area: 3,650 m²
Architects: Sauerbruch Hutton
Client: BM-Service
Structural engineering: Andreas Külich
Ingenieurbüro für Tragwerksplanung
Services: Kofler Energies AG
Fire protection: hhpberlin Ingenieure für
Brandschutz
Building physics: Müller-BBM
Timber construction: Kai Vater Zimmerei
und Holzbau GmbH & Co. KG
Photographer: Jan Bitter

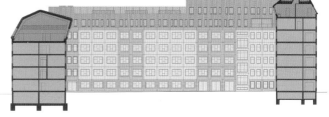

Berlin
23 Berlin Metropolitan School
Architects: Sauerbruch Hutton

The Berlin Metropolitan School was erected in 1987 in prefabricated construction common in the GDR, using the school building type called "Schulbaureihe 80": four building sections are clustered around a generous schoolyard in their middle.

The project envisaged rooftop extensions to three of the existing buildings and a lateral annex extending down to ground level. The room schedule included additional classrooms, music rooms, a library with access to a roof garden, administration offices, and a large auditorium. Variation in room size and quality now provides spaces that are suitable for individual learning and team-based work.

The construction work had to be executed during school hours and was realized in stages. Therefore, the extension was designed as a prefabricated timber system that could be quickly erected in phases. Owing to its own low weight, the timber construction did not require reinforcement of the existing foundations and supporting structure.

On the outside, the timber is clad with copper, which is complementary to the warm brown shades of the ceramic, brick-like surface of the existing building. On the inside, it is left exposed to create a healthy indoor environment for students and teachers, enhanced by natural and sustainable materials.

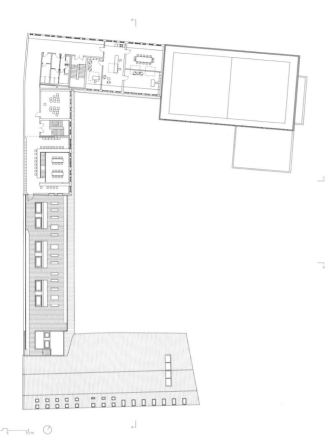

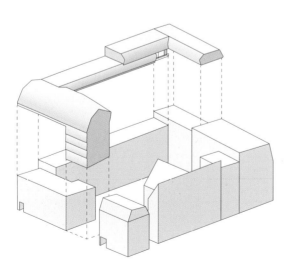

Location: Erandio, Spain
Completion: 2018
Gross floor area: 2,055 m^2
Architects: AZAB
Client: Basque Government
Structural engineering: Jon Bilbao
Building services engineering:
Unai Martínez de la Hidalga
Contractor: Roof covering Cyar
Photographer: Luis Díaz Díaz

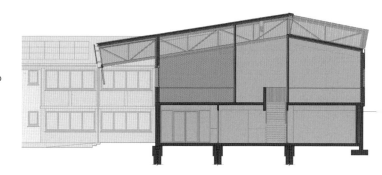

Erandio
24 Altzaga School
Architects: AZAB

The project stemmed from the need to reconfigure the uses and forms of the previous school building designed by architect D. Javier Fontán Gamarra in 1988. The main points of the project were to maintain the identity of the building and its volumes to the greatest possible extent, to enhance natural lighting, and to create visually connected circulation spaces. The intervention included the construction of new classrooms and common spaces, replacing the volume of the previous gym, and the addition of a new staircase with an elevator, to comply with current regulations.

The new volume was built by recovering the existing metal structure of the gym: the current beams were transformed into trusses in order to increase the span and position the supports of the west façade in accordance with the new circulation layout. The west cantilever truss partially compensates the forces due to the increase in span between the columns.

Given the importance of natural lighting for common areas and corridors, vertical skylights were installed to provide a bright environment, but with no direct light. Openings were also created in the ground floor ceiling to provide natural light and ventilation for the spaces

without windows. New windows were installed in the south wall.

The clarity of circulation and the use of bright colors are key design elements for use by children. The new metal volume fits in with the red brick building and expresses its independence through the change of material; at the same time, however, it creates a symbiotic relationship with the existing one. The new component does not overpower the past but stands in harmony, creating a new outdoor space, such as the covered atrium at the entrance to the school.

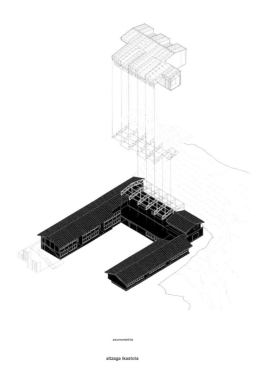

axonometria

altzaga ikastola

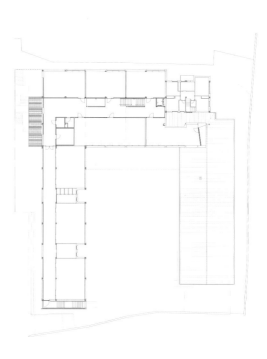

Bibliography

The roof as a livable space: architecture and imagery

Ambrosini, Gustavo and Guido Callegari. "Roofscapes: Urban Acupuncture". *Shijie Jianzhu* 11 (November 2017), 1–79.

Barbieri, Olivo. *Site specific_ROMA 04*. Roma: Zone Attive, 2004.

Busch, Akiko. *Rooftop Architecture: The Art of Going Through the Roof.* New York: Henry Holt & Co., 1991.

Cameron, Robert. *Above San Francisco.* San Francisco: Cameron and Company, 1969.

Campoli, Julie and Alex MacLean. *Visualizing Density.* Cambridge, MA: Lincoln Institute of Land Policy, 2007.

Canhamm Stefan and Rufina Wu. *Portraits from above. Hong Kong's informal rooftop communities.* Berlin: Peperoni Books, 2008.

Colomina, Beatriz. *Privacy and Publicity. Modern Architecture as Mass Media.* Cambridge, MA: The MIT Press, 1994.

Colquhoun, Alan. "Displacements of Concepts in Le Corbusier". *Architectural Design* 43 (April 1972), 220–43. Repr. in *Essays and Architectural Criticism: Modern Architecture and Historical Change.* Cambridge, London: MIT Press, 1991, 51–66.

Croset, Pierre Alain. "Il tetto-giardino: 'ragione tecnica' e ideale tecnico". *Rassegna. Problemi di architettura dell'ambiente*, no. 8 (1981), 25–38.

Dalzell, Rebecca. "The Gilded Age Origins of New York City's Rooftop Gardens". *Curbed*, July 16, 2014, https://ny.curbed.com/2014/7/16/10076106/the-gilded-age-origins-of-new-york-citys-rooftop-gardens.

El Lissitzky. *Russia. An Architecture for World Revolution.* 1929. Translated by Eric Dluhosch. Cambridge, MA: The MIT Press, 1970.

Döcker, Richard. *Terrassentyp. Krankenhaus, Erholungsheim, Hotel, Bürohaus, Einfamilienhaus, Siedlungshaus, Miethaus und die Stadt.* Stuttgart: Akademischer Verlag Dr. Fritz Wedekind & Co., 1929.

Fraser, Valerie. "Le Corbusier cannibalisé. Les jardins du MES". *Roberto Burle Marx. La modernité du paysage*, edited by Lauro Cavalcanti et al., 231–39. Paris: Cité de l'architecture & du patrimoine/Institut français d'architecture/Actar, 2011.

Gropius, Walter. "Das flache Dach: Internationale Umfrage". *Bauwelt* (February-April 1926), 162–68, 223–27, 322–24, 361–62.

Hénard, Eugène. "The Cities of the Future". Royal Institute of British Architects, Town Planning Conference, London, October 10–15, 1910, *Transactions.* London: The Royal Institute of British Architects, 1911, 345–67.

Koolhaas, Rem and Irma Boom, ed. *Elements of architecture. Roof.* Venice: Marsilio, 2014.

Le Corbusier. "Théorie du toit-jardin". *L'architecture vivante* (Autumn 1927), 13–18.

Le Corbusier. *Towards an Architecture.* 1928. Translated by John Goodman. Los Angeles: Getty, 2007.

Le Corbusier. *Oeuvre complète, volume 1, 1910–1929.* Zurich: Les Editions Girsberger, 1961.

Le Corbusier and Pierre Jeanneret. *Almanach d'architecture moderne*, Collection de "L'Esprit nouveau". Paris: Éditions Crès, 1926. Translated by Ulrich Conrads. *Programs and Manifestoes on 20th-Century Architecture.* Cambridge, MA: The MIT Press, 1970.

MacLean, Alex. *Up on the Roof: New York's Hidden Skyline Spaces.* New York: Princeton Architectural Press, 2012.

May, Ernst. "Das flache Dach". *Das neue Frankfurt*, I, 7, (October-December 1927), 150.

Martinez, Andrés. *Abitar la cubierta.* Barcelona: Editorial Gustavo Gil, 2005.

Melet, Ed and Eric Vreedenburgh. *Rooftop Architecture. Building on an Elevated Surface.* Rotterdam: NAi Publishers, 2005.

Nielsen, Morten. "Rooftop Autophagy. Vertical

Monadism in Maputo, Mozambique". *Urban Forum* 31 (2020), 311–30.

Oechslin, Werner and Wilfried Wang. "Les Cinq Points d'une Architecture Nouvelle". *Assemblage*, no. 4 (October 1987), 82–93.

Pommer, Richard. "The Flat Roof: A Modernist Controversy in Germany". *Art Journal* 43, no. 2 (1983), 158–69.

Pommer, Richard. "Revising Modernist History: The Architecture of the 1920s and 1930s". *Art Journal* 43, no. 2 (1983), 107.

Rabaça, Armando, ed. *Le Corbusier. History and Tradition.* Coimbra: Coimbra University Press, 2017.

Schildt, Goran, ed. *Sketches. Alvar Aalto.* Translated by Stuart Wrede. Cambridge, MA: The MIT Press, 1978.

Von Moos, Stanislaus. *Le Corbusier: Elements of a Synthesis.* Rotterdam: 010 Publishers, 2009.

Vertical extension as a strategy for the resilient city

Boeri, Andrea and Ernesto Antonini, Jacopo Gaspari, Danila Longo. *Energy Design Strategies for Retrofitting: Methodology, Technologies, and Applications.* Southampton: WITpress, 2014.

Bouzarovski, Stefan. *Retrofitting the City Residential Flexibility, Resilience and the Built Environment.* London: I.B. Tauris publishers, 2015.

Brown, Philip and William Swan. *Retrofitting the Built Environment.* New York: Editor John Wiley & Sons, 2013.

Dunham-Jones, Ellen and June Williamson. *Retrofitting Suburbia: Urban Design Solutions for Redesigning Suburbs.* New York: Editor John Wiley & Sons, 2011.

Eames, Malcolm and Tim Dixon, Miriam Hunt, Simon Lannon. *Retrofitting Cities for Tomorrow's World.* Hoboken: Wiley-Blackwell, 2017.

Gruentuch, Armand and Almut Ernst. *Convertible City: Modes of Densification and Dissolving Boundaries.* Berlin: Archplus, 2007.

Horne, Ralph. *Housing Sustainability in Low Carbon Cities.* London: Routledge, 2017.

Kramer, Sibylle. *Design Solutions for Urban Densification.* Salenstein: Braun Publishing, 2018.

Lehmann, Steffen. *Low Carbon Cities: Transforming Urban Systems.* London: Routledge, 2014.

Moley, Christian. *(Ré)concilier architecture et réhabilitation de l'habitat.* Paris: Éditions Le Moniteur, 2017.

Mooser, Markus and Marc Forestier, Mélanie Pittet-Baschung. *Surélévations en bois: Densifier, assainir, isoler.* Lausanne: Presses polytechniques et universitaires romandes, 2011.

Mooser, Markus and Marc Forestier, Mélanie Pittet-Baschung, Charles von Büren. *Aufstocken mit Holz.* Basel: Birkhäuser, 2014.

Robiglio, Matteo. *Re USA: 20 American Stories of Adaptive Reuse. A Toolkit for Post-Industrial Cities.* Berlin: jovis, 2017.

Roth, Manuela. *Masterpieces: Roof Architecture + Design.* Salenstein: Braun Publishing, 2012.

Stone, Sally. *UnDoing Buildings: Adaptive Reuse and Cultural Memory.* London: Taylor & Francis, 2019.

Talen, Emily. *Retrofitting Sprawl: Addressing Seventy Years of Failed Urban Form.* Athens-Clarke County: University of Georgia Press, 2015.

Touati, Anastasia and Jérôme Crozy. *La densification résidentielle au service du renouvellement urbain: filières, stratégies et outils.* Paris: La Documentation française, 2015.

Wilkinson, Sara J. and Hilde Remøy, Craig Langston. *Sustainable Building Adaptation: Innovations in Decision-Making.* New York: Editor John Wiley & Sons, 2014.

Wong, Liliane. *Adaptive Reuse: Extending the Lives of Buildings.* Basel: Birkhäuser, 2016.

Image credits

Roofscape design: an introduction

15   Rory Hyde CC BY-SA 2.0
16   Rob 't Hart
17   Gustavo Ambrosini
18   Gustavo Ambrosini
19   Paolo Rosselli

The roof as a livable space: architecture and imagery

21   Gustavo Ambrosini
26   Tony Hisgett CC BY 2.0
27   Studio Sarah Lou CC BY 2.0
29   J. Carmichael public domain
36   Jean-Pierre Dalbéra CC BY 2.0
37   Gustavo Ambrosini
38   El Lissitzky public domain
40   (top) amanderson2 public domain;
       (bottom) Dronepicr Luftbild CC BY 2.0
42   (top) Gustavo Ambrosini;
       (bottom) Julien Chatelain CC BY-SA 2.0
43   Guilhem Vellut CC BY 2.0
44   Fred Montwell public domain
46   Archive Gabetti e Isola
47   Kenta Mabuchi CC BY-SA 2.0
48   (top) Tony Hisgett CC BY 2.0;
       (bottom) Doug Letterman CC BY 2.0

Vertical extension as a strategy for the resilient city

Original graphics by Guido Callegari and Paolo Simeone, Department of Architecture and Design, Politecnico di Torino.

Case studies

The drawings have been provided by the designers' offices.
Red and black sections have been re-drawn by Daniel Diemoz and Samuele Folli.

Imprint

© 2021 by jovis Verlag GmbH
Texts by kind permission of the authors.
Pictures by kind permission of the photographers/holders of
the picture rights.

Cover: Cordoba-ReUrbano Housing, Mexico City. Architects:
Cadaval & Solà-Morales.
Photographer: Miguel de Guzmán

The authors of the texts of the case studies are Gustavo
Ambrosini (case 1–12) and Guido Callegari (case 13–24).
Maicol Negrello has contributed to the editorial coordination.

Copy editing: Bianca Murphy
Design and setting: Susanne Rösler
Lithography: Bild1Druck, Berlin
Printed in the European Union.

Bibliographic information published by the Deutsche
Nationalbibliothek
The Deutsche Nationalbibliothek lists this publication in the
Deutsche Nationalbibliografie; detailed bibliographic data are
available on the Internet at http://dnb.d-nb.de

jovis Verlag GmbH
Lützowstraße 33
10785 Berlin

www.jovis.de

jovis books are available worldwide in select bookstores.
Please contact your nearest bookseller or visit www.jovis.de
for information concerning your local distribution.

ISBN 978-3-86859-665-6